Exploratory Study on Responsibility, Liability, and Accountability for Risks in Construction

Prepared by the

Committee on Responsibility, Liability, and Accountability for Risks in Construction

Building Research Advisory Board
Commission on Sociotechnical Systems
National Research Council

NATIONAL ACADEMY OF SCIENCES
WASHINGTON, D.C.   1978

This report was prepared under Contract No. DOT-OS-60525 between the National Academy of Sciences and the U.S. Department of Transportation.

International Standard Book Number 0-309-02791-8

Library of Congress Catalog Card Number 78-64401

Available from

Office of Publications
National Academy of Sciences
2101 Constitution Avenue, N.W.
Washington, D.C. 20418

Printed in the United States of America

COMMITTEE

RESPONSIBILITY, LIABILITY, AND ACCOUNTABILITY
FOR RISKS IN CONSTRUCTION

Chairman

JOHN WURZ, AIA, Vice President, The Cadre Corporation, Atlanta, Georgia

Members

JOHN P. BUEHLER, Consultant, Bechtel Incorporated, San Francisco, California

WALTER S. DOUGLAS, Retired Chairman, Parsons, Brinckerhoff, Quade and Douglas, New York, New York

BEN C. GERWICK, JR., Professor, Construction Engineering, University of California, San Francisco, California

ROBERT A. GEORGINE, President, Building and Construction Trades Department, AFL-CIO, Washington, D.C.

JOHN P. GNAEDINER, President and Co-Founder, Soil Testing Services, Inc., Northbrook, Illinois

SAMUEL L. HACK, Director Office of Construction and Facility Management, U.S. Department of Energy, Washington, D.C.

R. M. MONTI, Chief Engineer, The Port Authority of New York and New Jersey, New York, New York

LOUIS W. RIGGS, President and Director, Tudor Engineering Company, San Francisco, California

BRAB Staff

JOAN D. FINCH, Staff Officer
CLARET M. HEIDER, Editorial Consultant

iii

BUILDING RESEARCH ADVISORY BOARD

OFFICERS AND MEMBERS
1977-78

J. Neils Thompson, *Chairman*

Bernard H. Breymann, *Vice Chairman*

Dan E. Morgenroth, *Vice Chairman*

Joseph H. Zettel, *Vice Chairman*

MEMBERS

*Bernard H. Breymann, *President,* Eco-Terra Corp., Chicago, Illinois

G. Day Ding, *Head,* Department of Architecture, College of Fine and Applied Arts, University of Illinois, Urbana

William D. Drake, *Professor of Urban and Regional Planning and Professor of Natural Resources,* University of Michigan, Ann Arbor

*Robert Martin Engelbrecht, AIA, Robert Martin Engelbrecht and Associates, Architects, Planners, Researchers, Princeton, New Jersey

§Joseph T. English, M.D., *Director,* Department of Psychiatry, St. Vincent's Hospital and Medical Center of New York, New York

Robert A. Georgine, *President,* Building and Construction Trades Department, AFL-CIO, Washington, D.C.

*Charles P. Graves, *Professor,* College of Architecture, University of Kentucky, Lexington

Paul C. Greiner, *Vice President, Conservation and Energy Management,* Edison Electric Institute, Washington, D.C.

*Robert Gutman, *Professor,* School of Architecture, Princeton University, Princeton, New Jersey

*Calvin S. Hamilton, *Director of Planning,* City of Los Angeles, Los Angeles, California

‡Cyril M. Harris, *Charles Batchelor Professor of Electrical Engineering* and *Professor of Architecture,* Columbia University, New York, New York

Lawrence E. Hinkle, M.D., *Professor of Medicine and Director,* Division of Human Ecology, Medical College, Cornell University, New York, New York

Morton Hoppenfeld, AIA, AIP, *Dean,* School of Architecture and Planning, University of New Mexico, Albuquerque

John C. Horning, *Manager, Engineering, Real Estate and Construction Operation,* General Electric Company, Schenectady, New York

Oliver H. Jones, *Consulting Economist,* Oliver Jones and Associates, Washington, D.C.

*Rudard A. Jones, AIA, *Director* and *Research Professor of Architecture,* Small Homes Council-Building Research Council, University of Illinois, Urbana

*Member, BRAB Executive Committee

‡Member, NAE

§Member, IOM

iv

Kenneth J. Kerin, *Director, Economics and Research,* National Association of Realtors, Washington, D.C.

Marjorie M. Lawson, *Attorney,* Lawson and Lawson, Washington, D.C.

Frank J. Matzke, FAIA, *Architect,* Springfield, Illinois

*Dan E. Morgenroth, PE, *Manager, Market Development,* Owens-Corning Fiberglas Corporation, Toledo, Ohio

Louis W. Riggs, *President and Director,* Tudor Engineering Company, San Francisco, California

Charles E. Schaffner, *Senior Vice President,* Syska & Hennessy, Inc., New York, New York

‡John B. Skilling, *Partner,* Skilling, Helle, Christiansen, Robertson, Consulting Structural and Civil Engineers, Seattle, Washington

‡Arthur C. Stern, *Professor,* Department of Environmental Sciences and Engineering, University of North Carolina, Chapel Hill

*J. Neils Thompson, *Professor,* Department of Civil Engineering, The University of Texas, Austin

Warren H. Turner, *Engineering Director, Equipment and Building,* American Telephone and Telegraph Company, Basking Ridge, New Jersey

*John H. Wiggins, Jr. *President,* J. H. Wiggins Company, Redondo Beach, California

*Beverly A. Willis, AIA, *President,* Willis and Associates, Inc., Architects, Environmental Planners, and Consultants, San Francisco, California

*Joseph H. Zettel, *Vice President, Director of Research and Development,* Industrial and Building Products, Johns-Manville Products Corporation, Denver, Colorado

LIAISON

Lee S. Garrett, *Chief,* Engineering Division, Office of the Chief of Engineers, Department of the Army, Washington, D.C.

Viggo P. Miller, *Assistant Administrator for Construction* Office of Construction, Veterans Administration, Washington, D.C.

Maxine Savitz, *Director,* Division of Buildings and Community Systems, Energy Research and Development Administration, Washington, D.C.

Donna Shalala, *Assistant Secretary for Policy Development and Research,* Department of Housing and Urban Development, Washington, D.C.

James B. Shea, Jr., *Commissioner,* Public Buildings Service, General Services Administration, Washington, D.C.

James R. Wright, *Deputy Director,* Institute for Applied Technology, National Bureau of Standards, Department of Commerce, Washington, D.C.

William M. Zobel, *Director,* Construction Operations and Facilities Management, Office of the Assistant Secretary of Defense, Washington, D.C.

*Member, BRAB Executive Committee

‡Member, NAE

FOREWORD

Early in the 1970s, the Building Research Advisory Board began to call attention to the increasingly critical situation arising from the failure to deal effectively with risks in construction. Risks to life, of bodily injury, to the health of workers and the public, and of property damage were not the only concerns. The risks of costly delays due to decisions made and decisions delayed, compounded by the increasing size and complexity of many large-scale public service projects, were having an adverse impact upon both participants in the construction process and the general public, which ultimately must bear the burden of any costs entailed. Assisted by small grants from the private sector, the Board was able to bring this situation to the forefront of discussion and debate, and this effort led to the sponsorship of the Exploratory Study of Responsibility, Liability, and Accountability for Risks in Construction reported on herein.

During the three workshops and the conference conducted as part of this study, many of the most critical issues now have been brought into focus and many sound suggestions for improvement have been made. Needed now is a concerted effort to develop action programs that will produce the needed improvements and changes in both public and private policy and procedures to the end that risks to be assumed will be more adequately understood, assessed, and agreed upon by all parties to the construction process, including the public, and that responsibility, liability, and accountability will be properly and equitably assigned and accepted in a responsible manner.

The Board strongly urges that this exploratory effort, which involved so many creative and responsive individuals, be carried forward by initiating a series of simultaneous in-depth studies that will lead, over the near term, to positive programs of recommended action. The Board plans to continue its efforts in the belief that the nation must find a way to resolve the complex issues involved and to realize the benefits that can accrue to society from technological innovation and timely and cost-effective construction that is environmentally and otherwise sound.

The Board wishes to thank the sponsors of this program, those who earlier gave their assistance*, the BRAB Committee, and the many individuals who contributed their time and talent as participants in the workshops and conference.

J. Neils Thompson, Chairman
Building Research Advisory Board

*Association of Soil and Foundation Engineers, Silver Spring, Maryland; Hynes & Diamond, Councellors at Law, New York, New York; Morrison-Knudsen Company, Inc., Boise, Idaho; W. E. O'Neil Construction Company, Chicago, Illinois; Sverdrup & Parcel & Associates, Inc., St. Louis, Missouri; and Woodward-Clyde Consultants, San Francisco, California.

CONTENTS

Chapter I

SUMMARY CONCLUSIONS AND RECOMMENDATIONS

The conclusions and recommendations that follow were formulated by the Building Research Advisory Board Committee on Responsibility, Liability, and Accountability for Risks in Construction and represent the judgments of the Committee members, based on information obtained from three workshops and a summary conference conducted during this exploratory study. The support for these conclusions and recommendations lies solely in the judgment of the Committee; however, the reader may assess the soundness of these judgments by studying the workshop and conference material presented in Chapters III, IV, and V of this report.

The Committee's exploratory effort resulted in a rather clear articulation of the problems associated with responsibility, liability, and accountability for risks and established that, in the opinion of a respected body of authorities in the field, these problems are, in turn, intimately related to the rapidly escalating costs of construction and the increasing delays in delivery of vitally needed facilities. Additionally, an overriding observation of the Committee, and one repeatedly expressed by the participants in the workshops and summary conference, is that the policy and procedural issues involved in assigning responsibility, achieving accountability, and establishing liability for risks in the creation and utilization of physical facilities are common to all heavy construction, regardless of type. The same business, personal, and professional traditions and business, financial, and labor relationships generally pertain even though on some projects specific traditions, principles, practices, and relationships can be more significant, depending on the type, scale, duration, and ownership of the given projects.

The Committee believes that resolution of these issues must become a primary concern of all parties to the construction process as well as to the nation as a whole if the societal goal of greater efficiency and effectiveness is to be achieved. To this end, it recommends that the dialogue that has been initiated be continued on a more structured basis so that its conclusions and recommendations can be adequately debated and positive courses of remedial action developed. Specifically, the Committee recommends that a continuing effort be initiated to carry forward the work that has been begun and to establish procedures whereby input from all parties to the process-- owner, designer, contractor, labor, manufacturer and supplier, insurer and bonder, the legal profession, all levels of government, and the general public--can be brought to bear in developing the needed specific recommended courses of action that will bring about a resolution of the issues and constructive change.

The participants in the exploratory effort identified critical problems as they have experienced them in the course of their day to day operations and have offered potential solutions to those problems. These problems and their possible solutions are reflected in both the general and specific conclusions and recommendations of the Committee presented below.

A. CONCLUSIONS

The general conclusions of the Committee are that:

1. There is no clear understanding and recognition on the part of all parties to the construction process that risks are inherent in construction--i.e., some are avoidable and some are unavoidable, but these must be identified and analyzed and responsibility and liability for them must be equitably assigned and continuously monitored to mitigate their incidence and adverse impact on the process.

2. There is no adequate system or mechanism in general application at the present time for clearly and equitably assigning responsibility and liability for risks in construction.

In addition, the Committee draws the following specific conclusions:

1. Delays that cannot be known or predicted adequately result in the greatest losses to all parties to the construction process but most particularly to the owner and the general public. Even predictable delays have a serious impact on the sequencing and efficiency of project execution.

2. A lack of understanding of authority and responsibility and a lack of coordination and communication generally exist among the parties to the construction process. These differences together with an adversarial relationship that often exists among the parties cause ambiguity or inequity in allocation of liability and increase the likelihood of costs in disputes. Delay and losses due to cost escalation and reduced productivity and beneficial use of a facility also may result.

3. Delays due to governmental regulation and control, when unwarranted, exacerbate serious losses both in time and money. These problems are magnified because of overlapping and sometimes conflicting mandates and poorly defined and sequential responsibilities, policies, and procedures of federal, state, and local jurisdictions.

2

4. Actions of public interest groups can cause serious delays, but mechanisms to provide for the expeditious and definitive involvement, consideration, and disposition of public interest concerns do not now exist.

5. The traditional practices of dealing with liabilities through insurance and bonding are no longer adequate because of the tremendous losses the insurance and surety industries have suffered in the construction market over the past several years and the diminished underwriting capacity of the insurance and surety markets (due to impairment of insurance and bonding companies' surplus accounts). As a result, premiums have become unacceptably high and, in some instances, insurance and bonding for certain types of coverage are unavailable regardless of cost.

6. Although all parties to the process are responsible for providing a safe working environment, accidents that could be avoided or minimized occur. In addition to the personal suffering caused by accidents, considerable losses are incurred because of project delays and because of costs associated with litigation, particularly of the third-party nature.

7. The costs incurred in dispute resolution are among the most serious losses associated with the risks and liabilities in construction and represent a nonproductive expenditure of time and funds. Existing procedures and practices for dispute resolution through litigation and quasi-judicial approaches are not responsive to the economical and expeditious execution of the construction process.

B. RECOMMENDATIONS

Because all parties to the construction process, starting particularly with the owner, must recognize the imperative need and assume the responsibility for a solid program of risk analysis and risk management, the primary recommendation of the Committee is that the following should be investigated in order to facilitate the implementation of sound risk analysis and risk management programs:

1. Potential for application of risk analysis and risk management procedures to the construction process

2. Requirements for and availability of trained disciplines and personnel to perform risk analysis and management functions

3. Techniques for identification and analysis of risks

4. Construction hazard analysis as it relates to safety involving all parties to the process

3

5. Delineation of responsibilities in terms of the parties to the construction process (including government and the public)

6. Equitable allocation of risks and liabilities considering the respective capabilities of parties to control the risks and to bear the liabilities

7. The extent to which insurance and bonding modes are available and applicable to the construction process

The Committee further specifically recommends that:

1. The responsibilities, practices, and procedures of federal, state, and local governmental agencies related to the execution of direct and grant-funded construction programs should be examined in order to determine and minimize causes of unwarranted delays due to overlapping, overlaying, conflicting, and poorly defined jurisdictions and controls. It is believed that such an examination can best be initiated at the federal level by individual agencies working in cooperation with state and local agencies.

2. An interregulatory oversight mechanism should be established (a) to identify overlapping, conflicting, and ambiguous requirements of federal, state, and local regulatory mandates, responsibilities, and jurisdictions as they impact on the execution of construction; (b) to recommend legislative changes that may be required; and (c) to streamline the regulatory process in order to minimize the unwarranted delays caused by regulatory practices and procedures.

3. Decision-making roles at all levels in the construction process should be identified and defined and the requisite responsibility and authority should be assigned in order to improve the badly disjointed decision-making process that now exists.

4. An analysis of alternative modes for procurement of construction and its management in terms of construction type, scale, cost, duration, and technical complexity should be prepared to assist public and private owners in considering the alternative best suited for a particular construction project.

5. In order to minimize the losses resulting from unknown or unanticipated site conditions, the owner should provide a thorough site investigation for purposes of bidding, contract negotiation, and construction. All parties should develop an understanding of the relationship of the degree of site investigation to the degree of risk exposure for all changed conditions. Criteria should be developed for the preparation of such site investigations as should guidelines concerning their application in preparing bidding and contract documents and their relationship to risk exposure and changed conditions during construction.

6. Contractual language should be refined for clarity and to allocate responsibility and liability both for known and unknown conditions. Currently used contract documents should be reviewed to determine how these instruments can be improved through elimination of inequitable or ambiguous provisions and language that potentially can lead to delays and costly resolution of disputes.

7. An analysis should be made of alternative insurance modes and availability of coverage in relation to the parties involved and to construction type, scale, cost, duration, technical complexity, ownership, and management.

8. A reasonable basis for economic assumptions related to inflation and cost escalation should be established for use in budgeting, contract bidding, and contract negotiations and provisions.

9. Guidelines should be developed for programs to enhance public awareness. Emphasis should be placed on communication of information to and participation by the public in decision-making at the earliest possible stage of project execution.

10. An analysis should be made of alternatives for expeditiously and economically resolving and even avoiding disputes that arise during and after construction in order to minimize delays and the need for costly litigation.

11. Mechanisms that will provide better communication and development of the team approach among all parties to the process should be explored in order to further minimize escalating adversary relationships.

12. Formal academic, industry, and labor education and training programs should place greater emphasis on risk awareness and on the potential liabilities inherent in the execution of construction.

Chapter II

BACKGROUND AND CONDUCT OF THE STUDY

A. BACKGROUND

The increasingly difficult task of dealing effectively with the risks inherent in construction--particularly in large-scale public works projects--is placing an ever-growing social and economic burden upon society and, thus, upon the individual citizen. This burden is reflected in delays or actual denial of vital services and in rapidly escalating costs that ultimately must be borne by the individual consumer in the form of higher prices, higher taxes, or both.

Risks to persons and property cannot be totally eliminated from the creation and utilization of physical facilities any more than they can from any other area of human activity. While the creation and utilization of all physical facilities involve risks, the possibility for and size of loss tend to be greater in large-scale projects that involve lengthy planning, design, and construction periods and have a long intended service life (e.g., mass transit, power plant, water resource development, and building complex projects, many of which involve highways and streets, bridges, tunnels, dams and reservoirs, harbor and port facilities, flood control facilities, sewage and water treatment plants, pipelines, and the like). When completed, such facilities comprise much of the nation's infrastructure that provides vital "life-line" services, and the amount of loss on any individual project can be tremendous. Thus, the losses frequently can be devastating to the individuals and entities immediately involved as well as to the general public and the individual citizen. Furthermore, the costs now involved in distributing the liability and accountability for the risks inherent in all construction projects are reaching such proportions that the performance of the construction industry is being seriously affected and the costs of adjudicating disputes alone are staggering.

These risks, their disposition, and the attendant impact on the future availability and cost of physical facilities should be of concern to every individual and organization connected with or dependent upon the results of the construction process. Of singular importance is the need to document and analyze the vast array of contemporary risk and liability issues and the existing procedures and practices for dealing with them and to explore potential avenues for constructive change and innovation.

7

In addition to the obvious risks of loss of life, personal injury, and property damage resulting from natural phenomena (e.g., earthquakes, floods, soil movements, and fires), the possibility of loss due to human error (i.e., errors in judgment, inadvertant omissions, lack of knowledge, the unforeseen and unforeseeable, and efforts to apply innovative solutions even to well understood problems) is ever present. Further risks result from society's rapidly changing perception of the short- and long-range effects of construction upon the environment and the physical and mental well-being of man. This is evidenced by public actions taken to regulate more stringently public safety, environmental impact, occupational health and safety, and major resource development. At the same time, there are the added risk dimensions of resource, material, and energy shortages and of price escalations, many of which emanate from outside the construction industry and even the nation's own economic system. Finally, there is the plethora of risks of a more subtle nature that arise from real disagreements and misunderstandings about the intended, expected, and delivered levels of performance of people and facilities and of the myriad materials and components of which the facilities are made.

The present agglomeration of laws, agreements, understandings, and practices for dealing with risks and liabilities in construction has evolved through many years of coping with problems in an ad hoc manner and, in effect, represents a disjointed mechanism for handling often very complex problems. Most current policies, practices, and procedures (e.g., professional licensing laws, insurance practices, contracting procedures, codes and standards, and legal precedents) have strong historical roots. There are those within the construction community who believe that all new challenges and changes can be accommodated through an empirical approach to the application of existing practices and procedures; still others believe the issue to be so complex and our judicial and nonjudicial regulatory systems so entrenched that only an expedient approach is feasible.

A searching review of the current risk and liability structure in the construction industry and a major effort to develop new and improved approaches to rationalizing and extending coverage of the process of risk assessment, risk acceptance, and responsibility assignment therefore are desperately needed.

Among the many practices, procedures, and instruments requiring study are regulatory documents; contract documents, including agreements, specifications, bids, bonds, and other instruments associated with procurement of professional services, construction, operation and maintenance; product warranties; labor agreements; arbitration procedures; insurance practices; legal practices; and, perhaps most importance at present, all of these in relation to increasing shortages and cost escalations. Finally, cost-benefit analyses must be made in the interest of all those who participate in and are affected by construction.

A major goal must be the achievement of public awareness and participation in setting acceptable levels of risk. It is equally important that the public be aware of the risks being taken and the potential for losses and the cost involved in mitigating those losses. It is essential that there be more practicable means for allocating the inevitable risks in an equitable manner in order to continue and accelerate both technological progress and improvement in the construction community's performance required to respond more effectively to public needs and desires. It was to explore these issues utilizing collective input from all parties to the construction process as well as expertise from other areas and general public interest groups that the Building Research Advisory Board (BRAB) conducted the study described in this report.

B. PURPOSE AND SCOPE OF REPORT

The BRAB Exploratory Study of Responsibility, Liability, and Accountability for Risks in Construction was sponsored by the U.S. Department of Transportation, the Bureau of Reclamation of the U.S. Department of Interior, and the U.S. Energy Research and Development Administration under Contract DOT-OS-60525. This report comprises a synthesis by the Committee of the results of the effort together with summaries of discussions held during the study (i.e., during three exploratory workshops and a summary conference).

Specifically, the report covers the following study objectives:

1. Identification of the kinds of risks inherent in the creation and utilization of large-scale facilities; identification of how these risks affect the planning, design, and construction of such facilities (including innovation in concepts, in designs, materials, products and systems, and in design, construction and management procedures).

2. Identification of the policies, procedures, and practices now generally followed that affect the assignment of responsibility to, the achievement of accountability for, and the establishment of liability among individuals and entities for risks that occur in the creation and utilization of large-scale construction facilities; identification of difficulties, mistakes, losses, and misunderstandings that arise because of or that are abetted by current policies, practices, and procedures.

3. Identification of areas where new and improved policies, procedures, and practices are needed; identification and recommendation of new and improved policies and procedures presently available; identification and recommendation of research needed to develop and implement other desirable new and improved policies, procedures, and practices.

The report also presents conclusions reached and recommendations made by the Committee based upon the informed judgment of its members. These conclusions and recommendations are directed to the study's sponsors as well as to the general public and deal with courses of action needed to change current policies and practices in order to minimize risks and to achieve greater safety, efficiency, and effectiveness in heavy construction.

C. CONDUCT OF THE STUDY

The BRAB Committee was appointed in accordance with National Research Council (NRC) policies and is composed of nationally known individuals selected with due regard for their commitment to assist in solving the assigned problems, willingness to devote adequate time to the work of the Committee, and demonstrated competence in one or more areas of expertise pertinent to the study. The charge to the Committee was to develop a detailed study plan, to guide and participate in study activities and render appropriate judgments, and to guide and participate in the process whereby results of the study were reported and disseminated.

The Committee met eight times (at four separate committee meetings and in conjunction with three workshops and a summary conference). At its first meeting, the Committee reviewed its charge and the goals, objectives, and scope of work of the study. As initially defined, the study was to include three preliminary segments, each of which was to focus on the problem and study objectives from the point of view of and with the primary participation of representatives of either the owner, the planner and designer, or construction activities, but with participation from individuals representing regulatory, labor, legal, manufacturer and supplier, insurance interests as well as general public interests. A fourth segment was to deal with the problem and project objectives in an integrated fashion.

The Committee determined that the complexity of the problem and the varied activities and number of participants involved in the construction process were such that more tangible results could be gained if the problem were viewed in the context of an actual construction project, similar to a case study in which participants could respond in terms of actual experience. The Committee believed that such an approach would facilitate the selection of participants and would allow each participant to draw from his actual experience and to document issues from actual situations.

Thus, the study plan developed by the Committee provided for a different construction project to be considered in each of three workshops composed of participants representing a balanced mix of disciplines and interests and for a summary conference. Chosen for workshop focus were an urban and suburban mass transit construction project, a power plant construction project, and a water resource development project. This approach allowed for consideration of differences and commonalities in different types of construction; the construction of publically and privately owned facilities; design execution by in-house personnel, consultants, or a combination of both; and the interrelationships among all the parties to the process.

1. Workshop

Each of the three workshops lasted 1-1/2 days and was divided into four major segments: an opening half-day session in which each participant was asked to summarize his response to a series of questions posed; a half-day session in which the Committee members summarized the comments of the various interests and an open discussion of the critical issues raised; a question-and-answer session in which auditors were given an opportunity to question the participants; and a concluding discussion in which the preliminary findings, conclusions, and recommendations of the participants were summarized in the context of the project objectives. (A listing of participants and the project description used to focus the discussions are given in Appendix A for each workshop.)

The workshop chairmen, each a recognized leader in the project area under discussion and representing the owner and manager interest, were selected at the outset of the project and participated with the Committee in developing the format and selecting the participants for their respective workshops. Participants were selected by the Committee from recommendations solicited from the principal trade and professional organizations, sponsors, and NRC units having parallel interests. Each workshop involved 20 to 25 individuals comprising the following mix:

Owner and Manager--Three individuals (in addition to the chairman) representing the owner and manager interest in the project area under discussion.

Designer--Three individuals selected to give the broadest perspective and experience of the designers in the project area under discussion.

Contractor--Three individuals selected to give the broadest perspective of the contractor's interest and experience in the project area under discussion.

Labor--Two individuals representative of the principal trades involved in the project area under discussion.

Manufacturer--Three individuals representative of the equipment technology involved in the project area under discussion.

Legal Service--Three individuals representing the most objective posture and the interests involved.

Insurance--Three individuals representing various major segments of the insurance industry involved.

Regulators--Two individuals representing agencies responsible for regulatory control of the project area under discussion.

11

The Public--Two or three individuals capable of contributing on the matter of general public awareness.

Auditors included at least five Committee members who did not participate in the discussion in order to be in a better position to monitor the discussion, assess its content, and assist the chairman in his task (Committee members also were to monitor and summarize the presentations of specific interests to assist the workshop chairman in summarizing critical issues and potential solutions); representatives from sponsoring agencies; representatives of policy-making agencies including regulation and control and legislative affairs of government, and representatives of NRC units with interests in the subjects under discussion.

Participants were provided in advance with the following material: a list of workshop participants; a statement of the problem (including background information and project objectives); a project description prepared by the Committee for each workshop giving general specifications of a representative construction project but in sufficient detail to permit participants to anticipate what risks might be involved; a graphic representation of the total spectrum of the construction process in relation to risks (i.e., from project inception through planning, design, construction, and operation and maintenance); and an outline of representative risk factors to be considered.

Each participant was asked to review these materials and, in the context of project objectives, to respond to the following questions from his particular points of view:

- What are the risk factors involved in the conduct of your activities that are of greatest concern to you? . . . What are the risk factors resulting from the activities of other parties to the construction process that affect your operation the most?

- What practices, policies, and procedures present the greatest difficulties in the allocation of responsibility, liability, and accountability for risk factors encountered in the conduct of your activities?

- What are those presenting the greatest difficulties in your operation that result from the activities of other parties to the construction process?

- Where do you believe the greatest emphasis should be placed in seeking new or improved policies, practices and procedures, and why?

The workshop sessions were recorded by stenotypist primarily for the purpose of assisting the Committee and staff in the presentation of the summary of the sessions and to form the basis for the conference program.

2. Summary Conference

Following the three workshops, transcripts of the discussions were reviewed and, in accordance with the study objectives, summaries were prepared by the Committee of the various points of view presented by participants according to the interests involved. In addition, the Committee identified five critical problem areas that were of general concern and that impacted on all the parties to the process. On this basis, the Committee organized the summary conference.

The purpose of the two-day summary conference was twofold: (a) to report to a broader audience the results of the preliminary workshop discussions, and (b) to focus on the problems and objectives of the project in an integrated fashion. Drawing upon the results of the workshops and utilizing the talent and ability demonstrated by those who had previously participated, the conference agenda was divided into two general segments: (a) reports by the three workshop chairmen and individuals representing each of the nine interests involved in or impacting on the construction process, and (b) a series of five panel discussions that focused on the problem areas identified by the Committee, followed by a general discussion.

In his report, each workshop chairman was asked to describe generally the project that was used to focus the discussion in his session, the critical risks identified and tentative conclusions reached. Representatives of each of the nine interests (i.e., owner and manager, designer, contractor, manufacturer and supplier, labor, insuror, legal services, regulator, and the public) were asked to present a summary statement focusing on the study problem and objectives from the point of view of their interest without regard for any specific type of construction project. Each was provided with a summary prepared by a Committee member who had monitored that particular interest throughout the workshops and with selected statements of other workshop participants.

Five multi-interest panels were established and charged with viewing five critical problem areas from the standpoint of the interests involved and, perhaps more importantly, in the context of the relationships among the parties to the construction process (i.e., the relationships of the public and regulatory authorities to the project, the owner to the other participants directly involved in the project, the participants to each other, and of the participants to the public). Specifically, the panels were asked to identify steps that can be taken during the various phases of a construction project to avoid or to mitigate risks and equitably allocate responsibility for risks and to recommend actions that can be taken to improve relationships, practices, and procedures and, that, ultimately, will lead to reduced time and cost and improved performance.

The five critical problem areas identified by the Committee were:

- Unknown Site and Market Conditions--Subsurface and other geotechnical conditions; environmental and natural hazards such as earthquakes and floods; inflation, material availability, labor supply; etc.

13

- Personal and Organization Competence and Performance--The
  capabilities and limitations of all parties to the process
  (e.g., owner and managers, designers, contractors, manufacturers and suppliers, labor, legal services, insurors, regulators, and the public).

- Administration and Management--Project scale and complexity;
  preplanning; control of participants in the process; appropriate
  and prompt decision-making; communication and dissemination of
  information among participants; etc.

- Allocation of Risks and Resolution of Disputes Under the Contract
  and Beyond the Contract--Through contract clarity and adequacy of
  provisions; administrative procedures (particularly as they relate
  to such matters as scheduling, change orders, progress payments,
  and approvals); dispute resolution procedures under the contract
  and beyond the contract; etc.

- Insurance and Bonding--Availability and alternate modes, project
  scale, etc.

Each panel was moderated by a member of the Committee, and panelists
were provided in advance with summaries prepared by Committee members
and appropriate statements resulting from the workshops. Panelists
were asked to review these materials and, within the context of the
problem areas identified, to address, in five minutes, the issues
they considered most critical (essentially the same format used in
the workshops). Panelists also were asked to give greater specificity
to problem areas identified and to recommendations for effecting
constructive change.

D. REPORT OF THE COMMITTEE

After participating in the workshops and conference along with more than
100 specialists in the field of construction*, the Committee reviewed the
information generated and prepared this report to disseminate to a broader
audience the proceedings of the workshops and conference and to focus on
the problems and objectives of the study in an integrated fashion.

The summary conclusions and recommendations formulated by the Committee
were presented in Chapter I. The reports delivered by each of the workshop chairmen are presented in Chapter III; statements by individuals
representing the nine interests that are involved in or impact on the
construction process are presented in Chapter IV; and material excerpted
by the Committee from each of the five panel discussions is presented in
Chapter V.

---

*See Appendix B for biographical information on all workshop and conference
participants.

14

Chapter III

WORKSHOP REPORTS

The reports that follow were prepared by the chairmen of each of the three preliminary workshops and were intended to give the conference audience a brief overview of the discussions as perceived by the chairmen. The workshop titles and chairmen are:

- Urban and Suburban Mass Transit Construction, chaired by B. R. Stokes, Executive Director, American Public Transit Association, Washington, D.C.

- Power Plant Construction, chaired by John Tillinghast,* Vice President, Engineering and Construction, American Electric Power Company, New York, New York

- Water Resources Development, chaired by F. J. Clarke, Lt. General, U.S. Army (Retired), Former Chief, Corps of Engineers, Washington, D.C.

---

*Delivered by R. M. Monti, Chief Engineer, The Port Authority of New York and New Jersey, New York, New York.

A. WORKSHOP ON URBAN AND SUBURBAN MASS TRANSIT CONSTRUCTION

Prepared by B. R. Stokes, Executive Director
American Public Transit Association, Washington, D.C.

Perhaps the most important thing to come out of the process that is beginning now will be the fact that all of the seemingly diverse interests represented here did, in fact, sit down together in common recognition of some very serious problems affecting the efficient and timely prosecution of large construction projects. That this represents the first step towards some possible solutions was the general feeling of the distinguished participants in the Workshop on Urban and Suburban Mass Transit Construction who were most articulate in presenting their viewpoints.

The workshop was focused on a sample project that is not atypical of many recent heavy rail transit projects around the country and took the form of opening presentations by each participant followed by rather free-ranging discussion. I believe there was unanimous concurrence that the two days of the workshop were informative and productive. Because the items covered in the three workshops are very similar, I will leave detailed presentations to my learned colleagues, the chairmen of the other two workshops, and will instead attempt to summarize, in my own way, the central themes that emerged during the workshop discussion and are important in viewing the more specific problems.

First and perhaps preeminent is the fact that all heavy rail transit construction is publicly owned, publicly financed, and publicly directed, and this gives rise to many of the specific problems. At the federal level, this has resulted too often in a tendency toward the "paralysis by analysis syndrome," the too frequent creation of agencies and programs that translate too often into external delays, and a tendency toward on-again/off-again financing and a shifting of groundrules once the game has started. At the local level, this simple fact results in an attitude that makes an adversary relationship redolent of litigation virtually inescapable. Local officials seem to believe that a public project is somehow immune to the perils and vicissitudes that confront others. I need not even mention the low-bid syndrome, which is viewed as the answer to everything from the procurement heights in Washington to the levels of assistant city attorneys, or the kinds of fiasco that are occurring (e.g., the Baltimore subway situation over which apparently no one has control). While I am frankly pessimistic about the prospects for solving the various local-level problems, it seems that we must continue to work at bringing true maturity to the federal level and the conduct of its program and at educating local officials so that they will become more sophisticated in their approach to these very complex issues.

17

The second point is the absolute essentiality of involving the public at every stage of the project, from concept through to completion. I am not talking here about minimum lip service, but rather about the genuine, positive involvement that will result in the best defense against external interruptions in the prosecution of a project.

The final point has to do with the psychology of what I call unfulfillable expectations, which perhaps stem somehow from the fact that we did indeed succeed in putting several gentlemen on the moon. What is needed now in rapid transit projects is a heavy dose of realism: realism about the time required to plan and properly execute a project; realism about the amount of money that is going to be required to complete a project based upon a very realistic appraisal of time, the state of the economy, and the kind of problems likely to be encountered; realism, as well as equity, in the assignment of risks to all the involved parties with a clear and firm contractual understanding by all parties of what those assignments are; realism in our concept of what is expected of the suppliers and manufacturers who will be involved in a project, particularly those that involve the advancement of the state of the art or an unusual situation and realism on the part of the manufacturers and suppliers about what they can expect to produce and when.

Perhaps these statements are bromides but they come honestly from one who has been deeply involved in one very major project and has the scars to show for it and who now is deeply concerned as an involved outsider and non-expert with every one of the interests represented here. In addition, as one who has been a disciple for improved mass transit for the past 20 years, I am firmly convinced that if mass transit is to move ahead, we must find ways to cooperate rather than litigate, to once again become partners in a process rather than adversaries in a court-room, and to concentrate on progress rather than on providing excuses for delay. Certainly, our energy problems demand nothing less. If this conference can move us one step closer to realization of these objectives, it will have been more than worth the time of all of us.

B. WORKSHOP ON POWER PLANT CONSTRUCTION

Prepared by R. M. Monti, Chief Engineer
Port Authority of New York and New Jersey, New York, N.Y.*

During the Workshop on Power Plant Construction, the responsibilities and liabilities of a $1-billion nuclear plant were studied. Many risks were identified, and it was noted that while many are properly assigned to the proper participants in the process, many attempts also are made to merely pass on these risks to someone else. These attempts may appear to be successful initially, but as time goes on problems develop, delays develop, court proceedings become common or at least a common threat, and, of course, costs keep increasing. The risks that will be identified below represent the views that were expressed by the participants in the nuclear power session.

The risks involved in the management decision process were noted as was the tendency to delay making a prompt decision. Of course, this results in many things including the delay of completion and cost increases due to escalation. In the nuclear area, great emphasis is placed on the risk of delay with all its consequences because of the many regulatory agencies, state and federal, and other groups that get involved in the permit and application processes. The fact is that approval by one agency does not necessarily mean the project is going to go ahead; it just means that the number of approvals required is reduced by one (indeed, a prior approval sometimes is negated during a subsequent review by another agency).

Also discussed were the problems that arise when design is incomplete at the time of implementation. The long list of necessary inputs from many partici-pants and the numerous permits and regulatory reviews of necessity result in a long period before design completion and, in many instances, it is found to be counterproductive to wait until the design has been completed to start the project. However, it was stressed in the workshop that one should be aware of the risks that are involved when one proceeds with less than a complete design and should be prepared, both financially and psychologically, to cope with changes.

Regarding the safety and physical welfare of the public and the worker, it was noted that some shortcutting of safe practices occasionally is implemented to gain time and reduce cost. However, this entails certain risks that must be recognized if all does not go well, and the amount of time and cost ultimately involved can far exceed that which would have been required if safer, more conservative steps had been taken. Again, this is a fine line, and a conscious decision must be made as to which approach the owner, engineer, or contractor will follow.

---

*Delivered for John Tillinghast, Workshop Chairman.

19

The workshop participants also discussed different site conditions, especially underground and geological conditions. The industry presently treats this subject using a variety of policies and contract terms that range from the assumption by the owner of the risk for unknown conditions to the attempt of the owner to pass on to the other participants all the risks involved, whether or not they receive compensation or have the financial ability to absorb the potential risks. Some agencies have adopted change-in-condition clauses but others have not, and still others are strenuously opposed to the adoption of these clauses. The workshop participants recommended that wide exposure should be given to existing practices and that each owner, prior to procurement, should evaluate the risks, including the insurance impact, and make a conscious decision as to which risks he should properly assume and which he should attempt to assign in connection with the unforeseen, especially geological conditions.

With regard to innovation in concept and design, the industry as a whole professes to promote innovation; however, at times it ignores the risks inherent in utilizing the innovative or unproven item and does not face the proper apportionment of related risks that arise. While the workshop participants maintained that innovative items should be included and that innovation should be encouraged, they noted that the risk is greater when the innovation is completely new and that a proportionate share of the risk should be borne by all in the process and not merely passed on (this was particularly stressed by the designers in the workshop).

With regard to selection of competent and experienced designers, there exists a small but vocal minority, especially within government, that supports selection of an architect-engineer on the basis of competitive bidding. The design process generally accounts for between 5 and 10 percent of total project cost but really dictates and controls the expenditure of 90 to 95 percent of the capital dollars. Incompetency in the engineering design phase can lead to inestimable expenditures plus a structurally unsound or unsafe project, which can result in tremendous cost and time overruns to say nothing of damages to the public and environment. It was noted that selection of an architect-engineer should be based on a multifaceted assessment in which cost is only one of the numerous factors to be considered.

Responsibility for quality assurance during the fabrication and construction phase generally is defined clearly and is assignable to the successful manufacturers and contractors. However, it should be recognized by all participants in the process that they can be affected by nonadherence to this prescribed responsibility for quality assurance and by inappropriate monitoring by owners and or architects and engineers. Thus, great stress should be given to this phase.

The risk resulting from inflation was discussed and, here again, it was noted that practices vary widely from the owner who accepts 100 percent of the risk and liability to the owner who attempts to pass on 100 percent of the risk and liability. Inflation will affect the economics of long-term projects in particular, and it was noted that very detailed analyses should be made and the owner and the participants should attempt to share as equitably as possible the projected inflations, which are very difficult to pinpoint.

Also identified as a problem was the timely fabrication and delivery of equipment by manufacturers. Generally, this is fairly well spelled out and assigned in the beginning of the contract process, but, of course, it does not always proceed as planned because of slippages or because unrealistic delivery dates were assigned in the beginning. The bidders will bid and attempt to perform on schedule but have very little chance of doing so, and problems, delays, law suits, and additional costs inevitably will result.

Construction labor availability sometimes is not considered. It has not been as much of a problem in the past few years as it was previously, when it was a common practice of owners to issue construction projects in a particular area without checking or evaluating the availability of construction labor. (Likewise, the unions at the time had a practice of artifically keeping the labor supply low and there were problems in properly manning jobs.) Discussion indicated that on large projects the owner, planner, designer, and local labor leaders and unions should confer prior to the start of the project to evaluate the types of labor and crafts needed and to agree that it will be possible to provide them throughout the particular project.

One owner risk identified involves court decisions regarding the value of condemned property. One can only estimate what this value may be as one enters into the authorization of a project and, of course, one must be prepared for deviations.

Another risk is that community action at any time may disrupt, delay, or entirely suspend a project that has been authorized and started. Great emphasis was placed on this particular problem. Among the solutions suggested was requiring organizations that bring suit to post a bond in the event that their particular claim is not successful and they can be made liable for holding up a project and the cost increases and problems they have caused.

Also identified as a risk was the contractors' practice of submitting claims at the conclusion of their contracts rather than submitting claims and supporting documentation of additional costs incurred as problems arise. At times a little game has been played: the contractors are late, the owner-engineers do not process the claims, and items that could be resolved quickly for relatively few dollars become a major disease in the particular project's successful contract administration. The result is that the project again is delayed, the adversary relationship between participants is sharpened, and the claims get larger and larger. As one nears the end of the job, the impetus to solve these claims and disputes becomes less and less and, of course, the courts and the lawyers move in.

The risks involved in competitive bidding, especially for public works, were identified. While the system is still very viable and almost mandatory, it was noted that one takes the risk of getting a bid from a not fully qualified, competent contractor and, given existing rules and regulations, it is quite likely that one may be obliged to proceed in award to him. Thus, one must be prepared with as good a contract administration as possible to still execute a successful job.

With regard to the risk of strikes, the owner to date has had little ability to eliminate or minimize strikes and their delays and cost implications. Most contracts grant a contractor an extension of time for delay when strikes occur, and some also take into consideration the financial burdens incurred due to strikes. The owner, however, has no protection against either delays or costs due to strikes. It was noted that owners should make their opinions known before agreements with labor are formalized and should advise the industry that inflationary agreements, nonproductive labor practices, jurisdictional disputes, and strikes eventually will increase the cost of construction and reduce the volume that would be available. On large projects, hopefully some kind of a long-term agreement can be made with labor.

The availability of insurance and unforeseen excessively high premiums were identified as major problems. It was noted that in the past many in the industry paid little attention to insurance premiums, which were just tacked on at the bottom of the estimating sheet, but this has changed dramatically. During the workshop, examples were given of architect-engineers' premiums increasing from $200,000 to $1,300,000 in two years. Stressed was the need to focus on insurance early in the project and to have all the participants including the insurance companies agree that the owner, engineers, and contractors have done as good a job of planning as they possibly can under the circumstances.

The risk of high cost due to design inflexibility was discussed, and it was pointed out that alternates are not considered or permitted. Owners and engineers were criticized for sometimes not allowing the contractor to use his ingenuity in the process. In addition, it was noted that it is necessary to have proper manufacturer input.

C. <u>WORKSHOP ON WATER RESOURCES DEVELOPMENT</u>

Prepared by Frederick J. Clarke, Lt. General
U.S. Army (Retired), Former Chief
Corps of Engineers, Washington, D.C.

After listening to the summaries of the other two workshops, I must say that it is very difficult to distinguish any differences in the liabilities involved in mass transit, utilities, and water resources projects. During the Workshop on Water Resources Development, we discussed a project involving a large dam, probably a $0.5-billion project, that seemed to have all the complications. It was on a stream that had some scenic value; it was above a populated area; and it was multipurpose in that it was going to provide power, irrigation, flood control, and water supply and take care of wildlife and recreation. It was publicly, probably federally, owned and was engineered by the agency but with consultants brought in for the geotechnical aspects of the foundation and special features. A multiplicity of environmental problems were involved, and one of our participants observed that there probably would be very few problems of responsibility, liability, and accountability for risks because this project could never be built in today's world and, even if it were authorized, it would be one of those on the President's list and probably would be delayed for a considerable period of time. However, we assumed that it would get under way and it formed the backdrop for a wide-ranging discussion that we believe reflects the magnitude of some of the problems that might be encountered.

The concerns that were expressed by the workshop participants seemed to fall into two categories: The first involves those risks that either directly or indirectly impact on the safety of the structure, and the second, those that present less of a hazard and concern the question of who pays for changes or happenings that were not expected at the initiation of the project. The distinction between the two groups is not all that clear since many of the risk elements that are involved in safety also raise questions as to financial responsibility for corrective measures. Similarly, the elements of risks primarily concerned with the question of who pays also may have minor impacts with respect to safety.

From the workshop discussion, it appeared that the problems of responsibility, liability, and accountability arise from euphoria at the initiation of a project, the feeling that everything will go all right and according to plan. This early optimism, often coupled with an imprecise definition of responsibilities, is shattered when unexpected events occur.

A conclusion to be drawn from the workshop is that practically every element of risk has some impact on most of the members of the construction team--from the owner through the designer, the contractor, labor, the supplier, the regulatory agencies, and often to the public at large. If the responsibilities are not assigned clearly initially and are not accepted initially, the later determination of responsibilities all too often requires legal resolution.

23

The most serious of the risks is that of undetected human error. These errors, at best, will require corrective action and, at worst, can pose serious safety problems that can impose very heavy responsibilities in terms of impact on the public.

The next most serious risk appears to be that of innovation involving the use of new materials or new uses for old materials. Of course, innovation is sought to save time and money; however, should the innovation prove to be unsuccessful, additional time and money will be required to correct the earlier judgments. In the worst case, a failure could have serious consequences.

The other elements of risk that were discussed appear to have less serious potential impacts. Most of them involve questions of responsibility and center on adjustments for payments. Changed conditions, particularly those with respect to foundations, were discussed at great length. The consensus of the workshop participants was that contract agreements should attempt to clarify the responsibilities in advance. The need for early consultation among the participants to bring about a proper understanding of responsibilities was emphasized, and there was a clear consensus that the owner of the facility is best situated to secure understanding of responsibilities before problems arise.

A substantial number of the participants favored some form of arbitration to promptly resolve disputes arising from unexpected events not covered clearly in contractual arrangements. While some felt that innovation was desirable, the majority of the group was conservative in its judgment that safety was the paramount consideration and that designers and builders should rely on tested materials and tested methods.

We had a lengthy discussion of the effects of environmental impact studies. While this discussion had some bearing on the assignment of responsibilities, it mainly was an expression of the frustration of most participants because of unexpected or prolonged delays in projects with attendant higher costs and, of course, ultimately the question of who pays.

While it is difficult to distill specific suggestions for changes out of our discussions, I think there was some degree of consensus as to the direction that change should take. Some of my observations focus on what I would call the "motherhood" characteristics: better planning, the responsibility of the owner to ensure that better planning does take place, and more equity among the participants in the project. It appears that most seem to feel the owner has the basic responsibility because the decision to build something automatically involves the owner in accepting the major risks, and it is only with full understanding and acceptance on the part of the other members of the team that the owner can pass on those risks to others.

The consensus was for a conservative approach. The participants wanted equity in the "changed conditions." There was a consensus, I believe, that third-party delays, particularly those involving suits by public interests that cause delays, have to be the responsibility of the owner because it is his job to ensure that they do not occur. Strong support also was voiced for arbitration rather than for going to the courts to resolve the differences among the participants.

24

Chapter IV

CONSTRUCTION PROCESS INTERESTS SUMMARY STATEMENTS

In order to demonstrate the complex relationships of the parties to the
construction process and the individual perspectives and concerns of the
various interests involved, a summary statement was prepared by a representative of each of the nine interests--owner and manager, designer, contractor,
manufacturer and supplier, labor, insurance, legal, regulator, and public.
These individuals were provided with summaries prepared by the Committee
members who had monitored that particular interest throughout the workshops
and selected statements of other workshop participants. The summaries
focused on the program problem and objectives without regard for any specific
type of construction project.

What follows then are:

- Owner and manager statement prepared by John Hoban, Deputy Director,
  Rail Transit Department, The Port Authority of New York and New
  Jersey, New York, New York

- Designer statement prepared by Peter Smith, President and Chairman,
  Gibbs and Hill, Inc., New York, New York

- Contractor statement prepared by George Fox, Executive Vice President
  Grow Tunneling Corporation, New York, New York

- Manufacturer and supplier statement prepared by H. Jack Hunkele,
  President, Foley Machinery Company, Piscataway, New Jersey

- Labor statement prepared by H. Allyn Parmenter, Training Department,
  United Association of Journeymen and Apprentices of Plumbing and
  Pipe Fitting Industry, Washington, D.C.

- Insurance statement prepared by William Cullen, Vice President,
  Johnson and Higgins, New York, New York

- Legal statement prepared by W. Stell Huie, Huie, Sterne, Brown, and
  Ide, Atlanta, Georgia

- Public statement prepared by Celia Epting, Staff Specialist, League
  of Women Voters, Washington, D.C.

25

- Regulatory statement prepared by Roger S. Boyd, Director, Division of Project Management, Office of Nuclear Reactor Regulation, U.S. Nuclear Regulatory Commission, Washington, D.C.

A. OWNER AND MANAGER INTEREST

Prepared by John Hoban, Deputy Director
Port Authority of New York and New Jersey, New York, N. Y.

Quite a number of risks were identified by owners during the three workshops. Time does not allow a detailed report on each of them; therefore, I have tried to group them into common categories where possible.

First, a risk common to all major construction projects is delays in securing approval of governmental agencies to proceed with a project. (For five years I have been a project director on a project that has been to the edge of the well about three times and each time it has been turned back for another approval. We now have $6 million invested in planning, 5 years of construction, 6 tons of paper, and no project.) When a project is privately funded, licenses or permits associated with various aspects of the project often must be secured at the local, state, and federal levels. When federal funds are sought by local agencies for their construction projects, a long approval process with many requirements is involved. The current approval process, whether it affects the public or private owner, takes an inordinate amount of time, which plays havoc with an owner's budget and creates a critical shortage in the services a project is to provide the public.

A number of approaches should be tried to alleviate this problem: A time limit should be established for the agency review of applications. To the greatest extent possible, one agency should be responsible for approving all aspects of a project. Clear guidelines concerning approval requirements should be published by government agencies. New informal requirements should not be introduced midway in the approval process because of the appointment of a new agency administrator. (It seems that every new administrator attempts to be innovative and, without realizing the impact, announces a new policy that the staff has to exact from the grant application.) As a solution to this, career administrators should be responsible for establishing guidelines and appointed officials should be responsible for policy direction. Finally, it is often difficult to determine which agency's set of rules governs the approval process. (I recall one situation in which it could not be determined whether an environmental impact statement concerning a new railroad bridge over a navigable river should be based on Federal Railroad Administration procedures, Urban Mass Transit Administration procedures, or Coast Guard rules, and all three agencies are in the same federal department.) Possibly, an ombudsman of sorts who would have the authority to resolve conflicting governmental requirements should be considered. This ombudsman may be required at the local, state, and federal levels.

Another risk involves schedule delays, liability problems, and disputes in contract interpretation that arise when equipment unique to a particular project is specified and designed. At times, designers regard innovation for its own sake as necessary to a project (e.g., this may occur in such

27

areas as railcar, station, or structural precast concrete designs) when what is required is continued progress in the use of standardized equipment and specifications, with true innovations first being studied, designed, and tested in a research and development effort. Also, a permanent mechanism should be established for the continuing review of contract terms and conditions.

Still another risk of concern to owners is the threat of labor actions, whether they be strikes or slow-downs to pressure contractors and manufacturers into accepting labor's demands. (One recent project involved four strikes by different trades, all over wage disputes, and two of the strikes lasted several months.) Increasing use of the arbitration method should be considered as should the formation of regional owners' associations to provide a unified voice on labor issues.

The selection process for consultants and contractors is an area that should be studied in order to reduce the risks associated with design and construction. Unfortunately, too much weight has been given in the past to a consultant's price during selection. It has been recommended that the initial choice of a consultant be based solely on his or her qualifications and the price then can be negotiated. The selection of contractors in the public sector generally is governed by competitive bidding laws or regulations that require contractors only to meet minimum qualifications. The use of a predetermined ranking system incorporating things such as price, experience, and financial strength should be studied to reduce the risk to the owner. Such a system would have to be carefully developed and implemented so as not to result in procurement abuses that would make competitive bidding mandatory.

The construction industry shares with other sectors of the business world, such as the medical profession, difficulties with regard to insurance. Insurance costs are rising very sharply, and some unique risks, such as working on or adjacent to a railroad, are almost impossible to insure. Further consideration should be given to having the federal government provide insurance for such risks at a realistic cost. The whole question of the benefits and disadvantages of wrap-up insurance should be re-examined. (While I think it served its purpose in its time, my feeling is that is has outlived its usefulness.)

One complaint often heard regarding insurance concerns the application of deductibles to individual incidents during the construction period. Perhaps insurance policy language might be clarified in this matter, and a statute of limitations on the designer's or contractor's work also might be adopted.

In addition to the delays involved in securing government approvals are those that may result when a local community or other special interest groups contest the implementation of a project for various concerns (e.g., concerning the environment, historical landmarks, equal opportunity programs, or route selection). This opposition ultimately can lead to a lawsuit resulting in an injunction against proceeding with the project. Any of the issues mentioned can be legitimate, and when a person or a group is truly aggrieved, his right to sue should be preserved. However, at times these suits can be over frivolous points, and a procedure should be developed to protect the owner from delays due to irresponsible actions. Some have suggested that the plaintiff be required to post bond against a court finding that the suit has no significant basis, and the owner can thereby be recompensed for the delays he has suffered. On the other hand, we do not want to limit the ability to sue to only the wealthy, and further study is needed in this area.

We have found that an early community relations program designed to fully inform the public is a good method of substantially reducing unwarranted opposition. Whether the start of the project is delayed through governmental inaction or community opposition, it does have an effect on how the remainder of the project process is conducted.

In order to reduce the effects of inflation or to meet a scheduled service need, the owner may try to expedite the design and construction phases. This can lead to contract documents that are not as definitive as desired and to change orders, disputes, delays, and claims. When a project is federally funded, the government should be willing to fund construction contract development while the approval process goes on so as to lessen the pressure on the designers to make up for the previous delays. The present practice of granting letters of no prejudice does not solve the problem since these letters place the entire risk of proceeding with contract development on the often financially strapped owner. This assures only that the owner will be partially reimbursed for all his costs if the project eventually is approved, despite the fact that the owner has taken the full risk initially in order to reduce future cost, a majority of which will be paid by the federal government.

The design stage, although accounting for only a small percentage of the entire project cost, has a significant effect on the entire project. This is where time should be spent in attempting to achieve the most economical design. Sometimes owners are faced with subsequent high cost because of the designer's inflexibility. One solution to this problem is to involve the construction contractor in the design phase in order to create constructive conflicts that will bring to the owner's attention areas where cost savings are possible. A tool in this process is the value engineering concept that creates bonuses for cost-saving ideas. A value engineering clause also can be inserted in construction contracts; however, the utility of this tool decreases further down the ladder of the process.

Another technique is to make the designer fully aware of the amount budgeted for the cost of his piece of the work (i.e., "build to cost"). Too often we set the designer to work, he creates the perfect design, and then we tell him it costs too much and to go back and redo it.

Inflation contributes significantly to increased project cost when delays occur. This risk affects owners, contractors, federal funds, and ultimate users, and no party should bear the entire burden of this risk. For instance, if owners as a collective group absorbed inflation costs, there would be very little pressure on contractors to bargain hard on labor contracts or equipment purchases. Yet, contractors should not be required to absorb the full cost of inflation since they do not have full control over it and an owner does not want a contractor to insert high contingencies in his bid to cover inflation. Since federal monetary and fiscal policies many times have a great influence in determining the extent of inflationary pressures, the government also should participate in escalation costs on federally funded projects.

There has been some movement on all of these fronts, but as with all the risks mentioned in the workshops, further study is required.

B. DESIGNER INTEREST

Prepared by Peter Smith, President and Chairman
Gibbs and Hill, Inc., New York, N.Y.

The engineer historically has eschewed liability for risk commensurate with his professional relationship with a client and has limited his responsibility to the exercise of due diligence and the skills normally provided by his peers in the profession. A departure is being observed from this "absolution" in that the role of professional service is being broadened and the engineer is being required to gird himself for risk-carrying liability regardless of terms of contract, traditional interpretations thereof, or the known intent of the contracting parties. The engineer certainly appears now to be subject to a very real legal liability to the owner (and perhaps to other participants in the process and even third parties) for lack of performance by any and all participants in a project.

The most significant liability risk factors within the purview of the engineer are:

1. Failure to observe his traditional responsibilities to employ the reasonable judgment, diligence, and care normally governing in the profession; to direct and supervise the effort with personnel reasonably skilled and experienced in the work; and to deploy adequate numbers of personnel to perform the several phases of work in timely fashion.

2. Failure to employ "all measures" in rendering judgments with respect to client options in such areas as load growth studies; evaluation of alternative approaches; counsel on mode of construction contracting; and forecasts of schedule, cost, and cash flow.

3. Failure, initially, to bring about a full analysis of all reasonable risks among project participants and to establish categorized accountability and communication procedures.

4. Failure to provide for all legal, code, regulatory, safety, Occupational Safety and Health Administration (OSHA), equal employment opportunity, and quality assurance and quality control requirements in design or to call for such observance by others in the follow-on project development.

5. Failure to adequately warn of or properly evaluate the potential problems related to an owner's risk in accepting an innovation in concept, material, procedure, or development.

31

6. Failure to provide adequate specification and contract conditions to guide manufacturers and constructors and to define interface responsibilities delineating proper accountability.

7. Failure to recognize incompatibility of vendor-supplied subsystems.

8. Failure to recognize inadequacies in manufacturers' data, to correlate them properly, and to keep abreast of modifications made (and effects on others' work) and of vendors' compliance with changing requirements.

Risk factors arising out of unforeseen external and uncontrollable forces are:

1. Modifications resulting from regulatory agencies' decisions during course of the project.

2. The possible government requirement to redo engineering-design if the budget is exceeded.

3. Delayed decisions by government agencies or delayed funding and committed staff.

4. Multiple-level government agency approved requirements.

5. Delays, preemptions, and disruptions of the design and the schedule caused by intervenors in the project licensing process or in actual physical progress.

6. The impact of discovery of troublesome subsurface foundation conditions undeterminable prior to site development.

7. The effects of delayed or the complete lack of vendor engineering or of major modifications during component or assembly manufacture.

8. Failure of manufacturers or constructors to properly comply with OSHA regulations, subjecting the engineer to third-party suit.

9. Exposure to suit by other project participants for the impact of delays and modifications.

10. Failure to discern manufacturers' inherent component engineering-design errors or inadequacies (although this has never been the responsibility of the engineer).

11. Failure to provide for the recognized operation and maintenance performance of the project after construction.

12. The impact of lengthy participation in public hearings on key personnel and on cost.

The reality and consequences of these risks naturally create a tendency towards conservatism in engineering and the preparation of parochial contract documents (i.e., the development of comprehensive performance rather than functional specifications). It is always comfortable and convenient to duplicate or extrapolate from known procedures with which considerable experience has been gained. Schedule pressures often dictate that course when an engineer is beset by time and budget requirements and penalties should he miss contract milestones or is subject to suit for an alleged "unreasonable number and amount of contractors' change orders."

Having said this, it nevertheless remains an inherent obligation of the engineer to introduce and exploit all reasonable, viable new approaches in design concepts and methods and the use of new materials, systems, technology, and operational procedures to achieve greater economies. He must predetermine that the new development will meet all codes and regulations; that manufacturers' claims for new products are valid; that certainly that project operation and performance will be improved. Manufacturers, vendors, and constructors must be adequately informed of the special requirements attendant to the developmental effort needed to ensure proper application and execution in implementation. Obviously, experienced, good judgment must be employed in evaluating such innovations and the owner must be made aware of the nature and consequences of the undertaking.

Today's projects are large in scope, sophisticated in nature, and involve many participants in both prime and specialist roles who all operate in an atmosphere characterized by indecision, delay, overlapping responsibilities, fragmented control, and fear of the unknown and uncontrollable. Owners often initiate polarization from the outset by placing liability on engineers, vendors, and constructors without categorization or regard to which or under what conditions faults may arise. In any event, the owner appears even more to demand to be held harmless in third-party suits—even for his own errors. The engineer extends the chain by preparing tighter specifications, employing every exculpatory phrase at his command, and inviting the constructor to nominate his best "sea-lawyer" as project manager. All this leads to the compounding of heavy contingency factors—where possible—or further assumption of risk by the implementing entities. (Our firm increasingly avoids public sector contracts imposing onerous liabilities beyond our reasonable control. They require one's analysis of risk absorption against a starkly competitive market with marginal profit allowance at the outset).

The proliferation of parties involved in development of a major project introduces further risk and considerable difficulty in assigning responsibility. There are often multiple levels of decision-making in an owner's organization, several levels of consultants and engineers, a construction manager and a battery of contractors, and often multiple insurers with prospective adverse interests. Attempting to achieve basic accountability becomes a major adjudicatory task often resulting in arbitrary judgment, commercial "arm-twisting," and total dissatisfaction.

33

The mounting problem developing out of multiple, overlapping insurance coverage of the diverse interests of owner, engineer, and constructor appeared resolved with the advent and acceptance by the owners of a wrap-up insurance program on behalf of all parties. The writers of this coverage now press for exclusion of the engineer's protection against claims from bodily injury and property damage arising out of the engineer's professional services--forcing dependence on the errors and ommissions insurance. The "shot-gun" approach of "sue everybody connected with a project"--especially in a bodily injury case where an injured party's coverage, through his employer, is limited to Workmen's Compensation--exacerbates the problem.

Ratepayers, shareholders, consumer advocates, and others are placing increasing pressure on utilities and public agencies to claim damages (including consequential) against manufacturers, engineers, and constructors for failure in project performance--regardless of the fault. The engineer's vulnerability is enlarged by virture of his role in performing quality assurance--extending his purview into nontraditional quarters--and, of course, his extended role in field surveillance. Insurance premiums, especially for errors and ommissions, no matter the degree of self-insurance and coverage are mounting rapidly even when an engineer never has incurred a loss. Cost of defense, despite the most remote involvement in a case, becomes a significant expense.

The rapidly escalating cost experienced through the term of development of a major facility and the important effects thereon of interest during construction, inflation, and other indirect elements related to time have resulted in intensive pressures to reduce the schedule period. In truncating any major construction program it is necessary for the engineer to develop a number of assumptions, especially governing structures, anticipating loadings that cannot be defined for many months (e.g., seismic values and ground response spectra that government agencies may well take years to determine) and postulating underground conditions prior to firm determinations. As these and myriad other determinations are finally made and significant modifications become necessary--or design modifications deriving from new changes in regulatory criteria or field-required changes develop--great stress is placed upon the engineer to minimize the effects on the schedule and the impact upon the constructors and suppliers. The resulting expedited effort engenders conditions ripe for human error coincident with diminished opportunity for review and checking and develops a potential for compounding the impact on the constructors.

It is extremely difficult to anticipate the problems that could arise during facility development over a decade much less the definitive allocation of responsibility and accountability among the parties. Definition of accountability also will depend to a great extent upon the owner's decision as to mode of contractual relationship for the physical construction (i.e., whether he chooses to be his own general contractor or negotiates with a construction manager; whether he selects phased or multiple bid subcontracts or a fast-track operation; and whether he elects a cost reimbursement, a fixed fee, an incentive fee, or a fixed-price or lump-sum escalatable contract).

Much could be achieved in mitigation of the incidence, and certainly the magnitude, of risks among owners, engineers, vendors, and constructors if it were possible to develop a definition of scope and of interfacing responsibilities as early as practicable in the course of a fast-track project. Potential unknowns, criteria assumptions, and suggested approaches would have to be identified and categorized, and accountability for risk and liability established and assumed among the parties. It is believed that this precursor effort and the initiation of communication procedures would be of considerable benefit.

Allocation of risks should be accompanied by a comparable assignment of authority such that accountability can effectively control the activity to the extent necessary to discharge responsibilities. Also to be considered is a return to a more "single-responsibility" design-construct or consortium mode of implementation wherein accountability and liability can be prescribed and through which more efficient joint operations with commensurate lower costs can be achieved. An owner should not demand that his project-wide wrap-up insurance coverage exclude the engineer's protection; this would remove the prospective adversary relationship among the parties and permit a freer pursuit of innovative systems and concepts. Finally, the owner should consider in any cost-benefit analysis of risk assumption that he alone can be a beneficiary if there is genuine accord among the parties to the project.

Reasonable liability risk limits should be established, apportioned commensurately with profit realization, leavened by benefits received, and mitigated by an appreciation of the conditions affecting the atmosphere in which the project was or will be developed.

C. CONTRACTOR INTEREST

Prepared by George Fox, Executive vice President
Grow Tunneling Corporation, New York, N.Y.

There is a growing consensus among the owners, designers, and contractors in the engineering community that contracting practices must change if the industry is to remain viable. When people who have been involved all their lives in major public construction say over and over again that something must be done because the risks are too high and dealing with them is beyond the capacity of the contractors, I think there will be a result. I think that the efforts of Subcommittee Four of the National Research Council's U.S. National Committee on Tunneling Technology will bear fruit and that contracting practices are going to change in this country because the situation demands it.

As far as the contractors' interests go, the paramount interest obviously is the public. There is something about the word "interests" that implies we are in different positions, but the public interest clearly must prevail. The public is entitled to know in advance the kind of structure that they are going to get, that it will be a durable structure, that it will be built in a given period of time, and that it will cost a specified sum of money. If they do not know these things with reasonable certainty, their ability to plan and to build for the future is very seriously impaired. Similarly, the contractor has to know just what his risks and obligations are, and they must be manageable risks for him or else his ability to function is, in fact, fatally impaired. I think we are seeking new risk distribution that acknowledges the public interest, the interest of the designers, and the interest of the contractors in getting major public works undertaken.

I would like to remind those who are not contractors of what kind of animal contractors are. And it is important that these major characteristics be kept in mind. The contractor is one who builds a precisely described structure within a definite period of time for a sum of money agreed upon in advance. The following significant attributes of the contractor have a controlling bearing on the issue of responsibility, accountability, and liability:

1. The contractor, after only four to six weeks to study the plans and specifications, has submitted a cost competitive bid and has been declared the lowest responsible bidder. All the aspects of a cost competitive bid system govern his proposal, his abilities, and his actions. This point cannot be emphasized too strongly; the community wants the benefit of a cost competitive system but is now imposing onerous burdens that make it unworkable.

2. The contractor signs what the lawyers call a "contract of adhesion," which is drawn by only one of the parties and which the other party cannot change in any respect. This contract is prepared by and for the benefit of the owner and is a highly detailed document that not only limits in every conceivable way the owner's exposure to risks of whatever kind connected with the performance of the work under the contract, but also carefully assigns those risks to the contractor.

3. The contractor prepares his bid by evaluating, in very careful and essentially mathematical terms, the cost of the various elements that are required to build the structure shown on the plans. These include materials, supplies, equipment, labor, subcontractors, insurance, and field organization. His bid is regarded by the owner to include added sums of money dealing with a long list of other imponderable risks and requirements of the contract, and when the low bidder signs the contract, he certifies that the cost of all these general items, which have a direct bearing on risk and liability, are included in the bid items of the work. In reality, contractors are unable to assign a dollar value to these risks and, in fact, never do so.

It is extremely important to keep in mind the above three attributes of the contractor because they bear heavily on his concept of his responsibility for conduct of the work, on his concept of his accountability for conduct of the work, on his concept of his liability for losses incurred in conduct of the work, and on his ability to handle and pay for risks that evolve from the construction contract.

An adverse role casting has taken place. Owners have drawn their contracts in such a fashion that contractors are responding in the same terms. The kind of criticisms of contractors referred to earlier are created by the very document or ambience that, although intending to protect the public's interest, creates a situation in which the contractor, for the sake of survival, must respond with the legalistic course of action he frequently takes.

Having spent sometime on the background and to call attention as a contractor to the critical risk factors identified in the workshop reports, the practices that currently exist, and recommended new practices, I will continue, leaning heavily on the last point.

I believe there are four groups of critical risk factors that contractors have to assume:

1. The risk of labor availability and productivity
2. The risk of subcontractor and equipment and supplier performance
3. The risk of physical and natural disasters (subject, of course, to the ability to get insurance)
4. The risk of strikes and work stoppages

These risks are very high and very serious, and contractors assume them when they sign a contract. These risks can represent a very large sum of money-- let us say, perhaps $10 million dollars in connection with a $20-, $30-, or $50-million job.

There is another group of risks that have to do with the owner's ability to move things along and to provide good documents. These are:

1. Completeness and adequacy of plans and specifications
2. Adequacy of funding for timely payments and to avoid delays to the work
3. Adequacy of owner and engineer staffing for prompt handling of approvals, changes, claims, third-party imposed delays, and regulatory impediments

We would like very much to have the situation improved with regard to these risks, but they do not represent major dollar risks. Still, I am not belittling the need for improvements--they are important, they do cost money, and processes must be improved. We must have the best set of plans, etc., so that there is no confusion, and timely payments are extremely important.

The group of risks that I think are extremely serious deal with:

1. The adequacy of subsurface explorations and the reliability of geotechnical reports
2. Reasonableness of construction schedules and availability of required work and storage areas and permits
3. Delays, suspensions, and terminations with resultant increased time and costs
4. Unforeseen economic factors such as embargo, shortages, imposition of material controls, and unwarranted Occupational Safety and Health Administration inspections and findings
5. Equity of contract terms, especially those relating to changes (changed conditions, allowance for escalation, and allocation of risk among the parties)
6. The development of an "adversary" climate on construction projects and the resulting litigious atmosphere

New practices, policies, and procedures that are needed are:

1. Contracts, including plans and specifications, that are written to clearly define the assignment of risks as well as to avoid the assignment of major uncontrollable risks to the contractor
2. The provision of thorough predesign investigations and reliable geotechnical reports with the owner assuming risks for changed conditions that subsequently may be encountered
3. Prompt recognition of changed conditions by the owner's field representatives

4. Provision for prompt resolution of contract disputes on an impartial basis (this could be achieved through a reduction of the adversary climate or by the mutual owner-contractor team approach or, that failing, by mediation, mediation-arbitration, or arbitration; litigation should be drastically minimized since it is in no one's best interest, not even the attorneys)
5. Areawide or project-wide labor agreements with the same expiration dates
6. Owners taking responsibility for delays due to third-party injunctions
7. Cost escalation provisions incorporated in the contract
8. Wider use of the federal contract terms used by the Corps of Engineers and Bureau of Reclamation
9. Specific contract instructions as to who is responsible for quality control
10. Owner procurement of required agency permits for construction and borrow pits, disposal sites, and work loads

I will conclude by mentioning two things that have happened recently. One is the experience with Eisenhower Tunnel Project,* where a project review board was utilized and which is a brilliant example of cooperation between owner, contractor, and designer. If that job had been done under the old climate as was the Straight Creek Project,** it would have cost $150 million not $102 million, and there would have been all kinds of fights. So far as I know, the job is moving beautifully, the owner is satisfied, the designers are satisfied, there is a mechanism on the job to deal with problems, and everything could not be better in an extremely difficult tunnel job. We should be encouraged by this example of cooperation and timely dispute resolution and we should look into its wider application.

The second thing I want to mention is a negative thing. The $800-million bid in the Chicago Sanitary District Project was absolutely predictable. That contract left no breathing room for the contractor for anything to go wrong. When reading that document you said to yourself: "The owner has you. He has got you tied hand and foot. You are never going to get another dime, and you have to guess your costs for the next six or eight years." In my opinion, the contractor did the right thing. His bid said: "If that contract is possibly what you want, our bid is not $400 million; it is $800 million." I think that bid will shake up a lot of people in this industry, and I hope some good will come from it.

---

*Tunnel No. 2 of the U.S. Department of Transportation Twin Tunnel Project under the continental divide in Colorado.

**Tunnel No. 1 of the U.S. Department of Transportation Twin Tunnel Project.

D. MANUFACTURER AND SUPPLIER INTEREST

Prepared by H. Jack Hunkel, President
Foley Machinery Company, Piscataway, New Jersey

I cannot help commenting at the outset that after participating in the Workshop
on Urban and Suburban Mass Transit Construction and reviewing the comments of
the manufacturers and suppliers at the other sessions I experienced a feeling
of depression, a mixture of frustration and almost anger, when I realized how
many obstacles and risks face major construction efforts in this country today.
It is not a bit surprising that a project can be completed in Japan in a
fraction of the time required here. I do not think our country really wants
a no-growth policy, but we are getting one, consciously or unconsciously.

In reviewing the specific problems that face manufacturers and suppliers, it
is convenient to consider two general groups: those who provide large custom
machinery, such as turbines and railcars, which normally is designed and built
to specific requirements, and those who mass-produce general purpose machinery
such as bulldozers, scrapers, loaders, and cranes. The two groups have some
problems in common, primarily their lack of a definition of the limits of
risks, making it impossible to predict the limit of loss exposure. I speak
of limits because some of this discussion focuses on where the risks are
going to lie, and it is important to work at limiting these risks.

In addition, the custom machinery group has some very special problems of its
own. Large custom machinery is usually of sufficient size and complexity that
it cannot be pretested at the factory and at the erection site it is dependent
on the equipment and systems of others. For brevity, I will outline a sequence
of the major risks emphasized by the other special machinery manufacturers
present at the other sessions who are more directly involved with this type
of product. In the contracting phase, equipment of this type frequently is
purchased through competitive rather than negotiated bidding. Many times, the
competition is foreign manufacturers who benefit from more favorable domestic,
legal, and commercial environments. U.S. manufacturers find it impossible
to provide adequate contingencies for risks that cannot be quantified within
reasonable limits. Some of these risks are:

1. Newness of design
2. Use of new materials
3. Changing design requirements
4. Project delays
5. Possibility of product failure
6. Inadequate escalation
7. Indirect and consequential demands

To bid with some degree of safety for all of these exposures would normally make a U.S. manufacturer noncompetitive against foreign competition. While there may be a limited opportunity to discuss contract terms prior to the issuing of invitations to bid, any significant bid qualifications or exceptions designed to limit risks automatically will disqualify the bidder. Most contracts protect the buyer to a far greater degree than the seller, and final decisions in disputes generally are dictated by the buyer.

In the design-manufacturing phase, there is inadequate cooperation with manufacturers during the writing of specifications to the point that innovations are incorporated that are beyond the state of the art and responsibilities for these innovations are placed unfairly on the contractor. The competitive environment encourages lower cost design and improved performance but does not give the manufacturer any protection against the risks inherent in creativity. Government contracts frequently are too inflexible to accommodate reasonable changes that would improve performance. And, last, it is difficult to design to targets constantly changed by regulatory agencies.

Further, for a variety of causes, the installation time often is delayed and perhaps doubled beyond what is reasonably possible and this measurably increases costs and risks. Among the causes for this is inadequate construction management, which fails to schedule and control the erection effort so that it is really on the critical path. Part of the reason for this is poorly handled interfacing with other manufacturers, contractors, and subcontractors that results in the delay, costs and risks of damage to the equipment with no mechanism for reimbursing the manufacturers for these significant increases. The regulatory process itself is, at best, indecisive. This results in frequent changes to the regulations being superimposed on existing contracts without a cost or time adjustment in the contract.

Project agreements with unions frequently are in conflict with the manufacturer's agreement and cause disputes and delays. Unfortunately, when a project loses its momentum, it continues to stay on low burner and in time creates all sorts of opportunities for new obstructions that make it difficult to get the tempo back and get it moving.

As for the operation phase, during start-up and operation the manufacturer is exposed to major failure risks in the warranty period and additional exposure of physical damage to property, whether that of the customer or a third-party. These risks, unless there is a special sharing arrangement with the owner, are being borne by the manufacturer, and while normally covered by insurance, it is highly questionable whether insurance to cover these risks will be available in the future.

With regard to recommendations, these risks and inefficiency exposures of special machinery and supply manufacturers should be brought within predictable limits by the development of the partnership concept, which was identified earlier as a replacement for the present adversary relationship that exists on a construction job. Part of that concept should be a deliberately detailed, greater sharing by the purchaser of the listed exposures through:

1. Fairer protective escalation provisions to cover inflation potentials
2. Better cooperation between the purchaser and the manufacturer in writing specifications and in preparing the bid invitation to make it possible to build-in reasonable protection for both the purchaser and the manufacturer
3. Measurably improved project management to minimize liabilities and attendant losses
4. Insurance provided by the owner on a project basis, including coverage for indirect and consequential damages
5. Coordination of union agreements

There is some dispute about whether negotiated contracts are better than competitive bids, but manufacturers like negotiated contracts.

At this point, I would like to bring together the interests of both special and general machinery manufacturers and identify a common problem that is probably our greatest single concern: the present legal system for resolution of conflicts, particularly as it involves product liability. Concern was expressed regarding: the high total cost of the legal process including interrogatories, depositions, and trials; the time that we all put in doing that sort of thing when we could be doing something more productive; the "deep-pocket" syndrome that makes larger companies fair game even when they have no responsibility for a problem; and the fact that the court system is a lottery because of erratic judge and jury decisions. Typical cases are too complex for most boards and juries. The theory of entitlement and strict liability coupled with the fact that the defendant, in most cases, is now considered guilty until proven innocent combine to result in unconscionable awards despite the facts. Most people are familiar with escalating product liabilities, suits, and awards and the commensurate increase in insurance costs, which have risen to the point at which insurance is either unaffordable or unavailable to many companies. This problem has to be resolved properly through legislation. In fact, there are two bills in Congress and a number of states have pending legislation to put a fence around this thing to some degree. The changes that most manufacturers and suppliers are looking for are:

1. Limitation of strict liability and tort
2. State-of-the-art defense so that something built 10 years ago is not expected to be built to today's standards
3. Statute of limitations to prohibit claims that a machine built 15 years ago was improperly done
4. Restriction of contingency fees
5. Definition of responsibilities with product alterations
6. Restriction on punitive damages
7. A product liability claim review panel
8. Limits on third-party actions for injury to the amount that the injured party receives from Workmen's Compensation

The product liability exposure is the biggest risk manufacturers face, and unless it is controlled, it will mean unproductive major increases in the cost of capital goods, the withdrawal of some manufacturers from markets, and the economic annihilation of many smaller companies.

E. LABOR INTEREST

Prepared by H. Allyn Parmenter, Training Department
United Association of Journeyman and Apprentices of the
Plumbing and Pipe Fitting Industry, Washington, D.C.

It is not often that we in labor are offered an opportunity to take part in conferences such as this. It has been most enlightening to find that, throughout the discussion, labor has not been identified as the biggest problem concerning responsibility, liability, and accountability for risks in construction. In fact, it is quite interesting to me to find out that the government, the lawyers, and the insurance people are the bad guys.

We welcome the chance to meet with those associated with this conference. I believe it has been good for all concerned to hear the problems that face each group represented. It appears that not enough of these types of meetings or discussions are being held and that the greatest problem we face may be one of communication. I have attended two of the workshops and found that there was a great lack of communication, thereby leaving hostility among the groups that bring about the building process. So often, the answers to questions of one section of our group have already been solved by another, but there is no way to know this because we do not talk enough.

Labor is not as bad as painted by many--not all good, but not all bad. In fact, we are seeking solutions to many of the same problems that confront owners, designers, and builders. Some of these problems concern safety and health, and labor can aid in this area. We have made many in-roads with the Occupational Safety and Health Administration (OSHA), and we have ways of training people that will give all the significant education that is necessary for your employees. You are going to find also that health is going to be the biggest problem in the long run. People have been worried about ladders and scaffolds and that type of thing, but I believe you must start thinking about illnesses caused by such things as exposure to asbestos and smoke inhaled by welders. These eventually are going to cost you a great deal of money, and we can help you in these areas.

Many of the problems discussed here arise before labor is involved in the job. I do not know how labor can help with the problems that concern special values, critical controls, or licensing procedures. There are so many things that labor has no control over, but when labor's part of the job is ready, we will do it and do it well.

Workers want to do a good job, believe it or not, and when a job is done more than once, it becomes just as frustrating to the worker as to the builder or the designer. It seems we always have to hurry up to complete the job the first time, but we always have plenty of time to do it the second time; I have never understood that.

45

It was pointed out at the Workshop on Power Plant Construction that often 50 percent of many jobs are done twice. Why? The quality control personnel are not there when they are needed because of engineering changes. Poor planning in the use of quality control personnel often upsets the morale of the workers until they wonder what is the use of doing a good job in the first place. For example, consider a man who is a welder. He has been tested. He is x-ray welding a 36-inch pipe, 156 passes. This man knows more about this work than anyone on that job, but he must wait around for two hours every time he goes around that pipe for someone, usually a junior engineer, to come and tell him whether he can weld the next pass. The waiting around and the wasting of time not only are going to stop the productivity of the job, but also are going to kill the morale on the job. There has to be a better way to plan these operations.

Labor is as much in favor of one-time construction as everyone else. Construction people still take pride in their work and, in fact, would like to be included more in the supervision and planning of the work. I stated to one panel that welders, for instance, often become prima donnas--the better they get, the more specific they get, and the more they want to do it right. If you know anything about welders and setting a pipe or seal, you know that this is so. Not everyone can design a structure, but not everyone can build that structure. Thos who build, those who pour concrete and rig heavy equipment, are professionals. All through the discussions I heard about the "professional this" and the "professional that," the lawyers, the designers, etc. Yet, a great many labor people are highly professional also, and I think they should be treated as such.

If labor leaders have knowledge of lead time on jobs and take part in prejob conferences, they can solve many of the problems before the job ever begins. I agree that work assignments on jobs must fit the labor agreement. Do not give the iron workers what the pipe fitters think they should do; that should be discussed before the job ever begins.

On jobs of the size discussed in these meetings, national union officers as well as local union officers should be kept informed. Labor is not an enemy of the building process; rather it is a firm ally if allowed to help with planning and with implementation of those plans. According to the experts, books that you people have written, 30 percent of the cost for a power station is the labor. We want to improve on that part of the project and help wherever possible in other areas.

Out of these meetings will come a report; let us read it and continue to talk to each other. So many of these studies seem to be considered finished when the last speaker has concluded his talk. We put down our "blue folder" and on Monday we will pick up our "yellow folder" and go to the next meeting and that is the end of it. We must not do that. Let us continue to talk to one another. Today I am talking to lawyers and designers and I like that. I understand things now that I never understood before. It is an education for all of us.

Labor people need to know about the cost of insurance needed for large jobs, the planning for the jobs, and the lawyers' fees needed. I am very sure that the people who build power plants--the welders and the fitters and the electricians and the concrete people--do not know that the insurance policy involved cost $1 million dollars. I do not believe that they understand financing--that they know when a job is held up for 10 days it will cost $4 million more. Maybe if they knew about this and the banking procedures and cost factors, they would be more receptive. They are smart enough to know that their jobs are involved, and they want those jobs, particularly now when unemployment is still high in the construction industry. (In the New England area, for example, it is as high as 60 percent, and those people are looking for ways to get back to work.) I am sure they would listen to these problems, and they should know about them. Now only high-level union people are aware of this information, and I think if the rest were told and we did some more communicating, it certainly would be helpful.

Labor sometimes acts like a private club. We know what we can do, but we never tell anyone else about the good things we can do. We have done many good things for the country, but, of course, building a home with free labor for deaf children is not a news item and putting a picket line around a job is. We can do things, and we can do them well if we understand the problems. I know I understand more by coming to these meetings, and I hope that some of you will understand more too and that we can talk at the local levels wherever jobs are. If we have the lead time, the proper people will be there. Negotiations should be done properly. At one discussion, one of my labor colleagues said that negotiation should be strong for the management side; maybe it is not strong enough. I have participated in some BRAB activities concerning building, and many participants say that sometimes they could not fire people. I have been foreman on many jobs and I have fired people--stewards and anybody else who could not or would not do the job. If that is not properly stated in the agreement, then maybe it is the contractor's fault. It has got to be there; you have the right to do the things necessary to operate that job and to have control.

Some of us have never talked to each other about our problems, and now we are doing just that. We have been able to cross lines. I came here this morning and sat with a lawyer and we talked on common terms. A few years ago, I do not know if he would have even talked to me or I to him. But the process is going to work, and I think that we should not put the "blue folder" down. I will do all I can to bring about the changes that we need to help our industry. So let us not blame each other for our problems and have that hostility. I have been fortunate enough to work with all of you here, all highly professional. I believe labor people are professional also. Let us continue our communication and get our job done.

F. INSURANCE INTEREST

Prepared by William Cullen, Vice President
Johnson and Higgins, New York, N.Y.

The consensus of the insurance people attending the preliminary workshop dealing with responsibility, liability, and accountability for risks in construction can be reduced to a simplistic term, "proper management of risk." Like all solutions, simple solutions invariably have a complex explanation. Let me assure you that insurance does not vary from the norm and, in fact, may very well be the frontrunner in the complexity race.

The first point requiring explanation is that the word "risk," when used in insurance, has a special meaning because the adjective "pure" is used, and "pure risk" is defined to mean only a chance of loss or no loss at all. In insurance, the other definition of "risk," a chance of gain or of loss, is not applicable, and any risk bearing such elements is not considered a risk. Therefore, we have a problem at the outset with most people.

Stemming from the proper management of pure risk is a myriad of problems ranging from the recognition of risks and the assignment of values to them, to what to do about them. For example, should risks be self-assumed or transferred to a risk taker? If the latter, is there a risk-taker insurance company available and at what cost? Within the nucleus of these broad considerations, workshop members commented on specific concerns. The insurance company representatives were concerned about inadequate premiums for the risks assumed on very large construction projects that often last up to 10 years and are full of many unknowns, many far greater than was contemplated at the outset of the project. Let me give you a concrete example: In 1971 when the Washington Metropolitan Area Transit Authority put into effect its coordinated insurance program, the District of Columbia Workmen's Compensation maximum weekly benefit was $70 a week with a lifetime maximum of $24,000 for any injury. Today, the benefit is $342 a week without a maximum limit. In fact, there has been at least one claim thus far that has a benefit amount exceeding $1 million for an injured workman.

Needless to say, no insurance actuary, whether he be supported by the most sophisticated computer or a crystal ball or both, is capable of establishing rates at the outset that cover all contingencies. Long-term jumbo contracts also impact on surety bond underwriters since these contracts are full of the same unknowns that make usual underwriting guidelines impractical. In addition, surety companies have a sociopolitical problem arising from pressures to provide bonds for small and minority contractors who, by usual underwriting standards, cannot qualify. Some years ago, an attempt was made to solve this problem through the surety bond guarantee program with Small Business Administration. While many bonds have been provided, many people do not realize that over

$70 million in net losses have been passed on to the taxpaying public through this program. Yet this program is not enough to suit the wishes of certain pressure groups and elected representatives, and they have conceived a new kind of thinking. Every contractor has the right to have a surety find him qualified to perform a given contract. One state is considering having the state insurance fund write surety risk, no doubt, for any and all applicant contractors. At least two other states are considering surety on an assigned risk basis, similar to the automobile assigned risk plan. And last but not least, there are several proposals before Congress or in the White House considering additional federal involvement in the surety business.

Other workshop participants expressed concern about different areas, but all seemed to dwell on one point--the availability of market or, to use a fiscal term, the shortage of risk capital. Virtually every workshop participant who had one or more comments in criticism of the insurance industry mentioned the availability or lack of market. Rebuttals ranged from justification of tight market conditions because of horrendous underwriting losses in 1974, 1975, and 1976 that right now total about $10 billion (and I cannot imagine any profit venture that can continue to suffer losses of this sort) to owner's contract terms being foisted on contractors by owners, to cumbersome change order procedures and payout schedules, and to the failure of the owner to recognize that he, too, has risks that must be retained and not passed on to contractors or insurance companies.

Several representatives mentioned the somewhat innovative (although not new) concept of risk management as a solution to the problem of cost and availability of insurance. Briefly, this concept requires the owner to place himself firmly in the driver's seat and to make a determination of his risk and loss potential and develop a policy of what to do about them. The risk management process requires: (1) identification and analysis of risk of accidental loss, (2) development of methods of treating risks, (3) selection of the best method for coping with the risk, (4) implementation of the best method, and (5) monitoring the results to make adjustments if necessary.

Once the owner has analyzed his risk, the specific techniques of risk management may be utilized. These are avoidance, retention, prevention, and transfer. Among insurance professionals, there is agreement that utilization of risk management principles by owners and the incorporation of such principles into the design of projects will go a long way in relieving some of the pressures on the insurance market as well as in decreasing the cost of insurance.

Workshop participants also discussed the modes of insurance. There seems to be some disagreement, usually where there is a vested interest, about whether owner-controlled or wrap-up insurance is the only way to go. Several recent studies indicate that wrap-up seems to offer many advantages over conventional insurance, particularly in reduced cost and market availability. On jumbo contracts involving hundreds or even thousands of prime contractors, subcontractors, and sub-subcontractors, the underwriting capacity of the world insurance market is just not large enough to provide all the necessary policies and amounts of coverage for all the contractors involved, thus leaving wrap-up as the only sensible solution if the project is to be insured.

In summary, I believe all workshop participants agreed that there is a capacity crunch in the insurance business brought on by increases in the number and inflation-impacted amounts of claims compounded by several consecutive years of underwriting losses. But the situation is not hopeless. There are solutions, innovative and tradition-shaking, and whether involving the owner, the contractor, labor, the legal profession (particularly in the tort area), or the public, the solutions require a break with the past if risks are to be insured.

G. LEGAL INTEREST

Prepared by W. Stell Huie
Huie, Sterne, Brown and Ide, Atlanta, Ga.

In reviewing the various papers prepared by the lawyers who participated in the various workshops, I found that their interests coincided, to a great degree, with the interests of those whom they primarily represented. Since these lawyers represented owners, builders, designers, regulatory bodies (and in some governmental agencies they were regulators as well as owners), and contractors and subcontractors of various varieties, it is very difficult to suggest that there is a consensus among the lawyers for the entire cadre of interests they represent. But there are, perhaps, some threads of interest that are common to lawyers representing the members of this group, which perhaps do not take quite as much of an industry perspective as have the other presentations here today. As a matter of fact, I think we lawyers look upon this matter of allocation of risk as something philosophical. Indeed, our training and our common law heritage tells us that the allocation of risk has been one of the major problems with which our forefathers have wrestled through the years from the town councils and the tribal chieftans down to today with our sophisticated boards of contract appeals and specialized courts and general courts. The issue of allocation has been the problem. Shall it fall upon the one who is best able to pay, or shall it fall upon the one who is at fault? Should there be some division of liability on a no-fault basis between those participating in the project? Should there be allowed monetary limitations on fault, no matter how it is to be allocated? So it basically is a philosophical problem that can be handled in the context in which we are dealing in one of several ways. Obviously, by contract there may be a shifting of risk. In some instances, however, legislation may be required to shift the risk.

We have looked at those risks that are governed or controlled, to some extent, by some members of this package of actors in the contracting industry, and we have looked at those uncontrolled and unforeseen risks. And I think most of us would agree that the ultimate liability is upon the owner--the person or entity that is going to remain with the project after the designers, contractors, etc., have gone. In recognition of that fact, owners generally try, as has already been suggested here today in many specific instances, to shift that risk to somebody else to the degree that is possible. One of the major factors in this is bargaining power. As lawyers, we have been very concerned that our client's bargaining position at the table results in their assuming risks that they simply should not assume and, in many instances, assuming risks that they simply do not understand they are assuming. And it is probably bargaining power, not who controls a risk more than anybody else in a group, that really, in the final analysis, makes the difference. It depends, of course, on the climate in the construction industry. In Atlanta, we had a major downturn in construction, and I have seen contractors assume risks that six or seven years ago they would not ever have considered assuming.

53

When risk is allocated, the problem is making sure that it is clearly spelled out in the contract document. But in this instance, even if it is clear, there sometimes are statutory limitations upon the assignment of liability among the group (e.g., the contracting industry has moved toward legislation in many states that prohibits the allocation of risk to the contractor for somebody else's negligence). The attempts to legislate in this area have had something of a boomerang effect as the courts have interpreted these limitations on liability; they have gone a little further than some of us had thought they would and have said that, in some instances, certain statutes mean you not only cannot shift the risk, but you also cannot limit it monetarily. This is an unfortunate problem. Obviously, the prompt and equitable resolution of disputes is the goal we all seek, and field resolutions, I think we as lawyers agree, are the best. Arbitration, mediation, and other extra-judicial resolutions are, in some instances, exceedingly good. Some of them are built into the contract, and some of them are available to the parties outside the contract. But one of the problems we have perceived is the business of arbitration panels and the special boards that have been created through the years to solve special problems in the contracting industry becoming more and more like courts. Their procedures are becoming much more complex, the lawyers are becoming much more involved than they were in the past, and the whole thing is taking on more of the adversary relationship that many of us have bemoaned here today. We are concerned also about the losses to all of us occasioned by delay. While we recognize that some of the delay is lawyer-caused, we submit that in most cases it is failure to use counsel in a proper way (i.e., as a counselor, as an advisor, and as a tool rather than as a weapon at another point in the process) that has resulted in delays that otherwise could have been avoided.

Judicial reform? Yes! We have talked about the spurious lawsuit, the malicious lawsuit, and we have been concerned that some plaintiffs do not have to post bond. Most of the time, however, the problem is with the particular judge who has it within his discretion to require bond or some other security or to dismiss the lawsuit. In Atlanta recently we almost were stopped in an environmental case. After we had won it, the plaintiff sought to have the court grant a supersedeas to stop the effect of the order in our favor pending the appeal. We, in that instance, moved for bond or dismissal, and the plaintiff quickly withdrew his request.

Another area of concern to us is the movement into an adversary position of some regulatory bodies. In some states, regulatory commissions are insisting that public entities bring lawsuits in some areas that may have an effect on the rate-making power of that body and, consequently, are pushing the parties into litigation that is otherwise unwanted and very risky and the benefits of which are very remote.

The cost of litigation is something that concerns all of us. I can simply say that the increased complexity of what is happening in design and construction necessarily makes litigation more complex and, therefore, more costly. One thing we have done in this country is to put too small a price tag on justice.

In almost every state in the union, less than 1 percent of that state's budget goes for the court system. We do not pay judges enough to get the calibre of man on the bench that we need. A good judge can control the cost of litigation; he can control the lawyers. I submit to you that while we need to approach this thing from the standpoint of judicial reform and legislative reform, we have it within our power to improve the quality of justice and reduce its cost substantially by simply putting a better man on the bench.

Prepared by Celia Epting, Staff Specialist
League of Women Voters, Washington, D.C.

I will paraphrase the issues to which the participants representing the public interest were asked to respond: What risk factors associated with large-scale construction projects are of greatest concern to citizens? What current policies and procedures followed in a construction process most affect the public's operation (i.e., the ability of citizens to be informed of and to evaluate risks that will affect them personally)? How can these policies and procedures be improved to allow greater citizen participation?

To purport to speak for a broad general sector of society on any matter is perilous. It is more so when one presumes to represent the informed citizen because citizens who are both concerned and informed frequently arrive at diametrically opposed conclusions on any given issue. This is especially true when determining risks and making safety judgments because risks and degrees of risk, as well as safety and degrees of safety, evolve according to individual perception and personal and social standards of acceptability.

How people perceive and accept risks also is a major factor in their actions. We all have a natural desire to minimize personal risks. Estimating, evaluating, and reducing our risks, however, has been made vastly more difficult because of rapid and complex technological advances. Merely keeping abreast of all the risks that may affect us is a full-time task. Increasingly, we find policymakers and bureaucrats determining what risks are acceptable to the general public. Should they be? I will get to that in a minute.

Summarizing some of the risks enumerated in the workshops, I came up with the following list:

1. The potential loss of human life (e.g., from the collapse of a dam that has been ill-sited or ill-designed or a nuclear power plant that has been constructed near a fault line)
2. Total or even partial community dislocation and loss of livelihood through land condemnation or, in the case of water resource projects, the inundation of prime agricultural farmland, valuable forests and woodlands, and fishing grounds
3. The destruction of wildlife habitats, historically significant sites, and water courses that provide unique recreational opportunities
4. An increase in water pollution and the potential for ecological damage through thermal discharge and increased sedimentation flows, etc.
5. An increase in air pollution
6. An increase in traffic resulting in the need for support facilities during the construction phase or sometimes throughout the life of a project

7. Fiscal impacts (including the operating as well as the construction costs of a project)
8. Disruption of community services, health facilities, public law enforcement, and housing caused by the influx of construction workers in a community

Of course, some of these risk factors also could be considered factors of benefit, depending on one's point of view, and this list certainly does not include any surprises. All of you here know that some of these may be the risks from the outset of any project. The point is that these risks also should be properly identified for the public at the outset of a project. As an example, there have been occasions when preliminary environmental impact statements issued on a project do not present a comprehensive picture of the project's potential impacts. After the project is approved and construction begins, subsequent studies are released that provide more details, making the impacts seem greater, but the momentum to complete the project then is in full swing and there sometimes is resistance to citizen queries or objections.

One of the most important risks to the public that I did not include above is the risk of the unknown--of citizens not being informed well enough to make adequate and accurate decisions regarding risks. On the other side of the coin is another problem--technological solutions for dealing with hazards often may be inadequate without a knowledge of how they will affect individual decision making. We currently know little about how the public reacts to scientific technological information concerning risks or about modes of communicating risk information. Perceived risk may greatly depend on the way in which relevant information is presented to the public. Earlier I questioned whether policymakers and bureaucrats should be determining what risks are acceptable to the public. My answer to that question is a qualified "yes" if there has been adequate provision for citizen participation in that determination. Citizens often are excluded from risk determinations because experts and professionals feel the public is not equipped with the proper expertise to decide what risks there are and whether these are acceptable.

The fact is that risk determination involves both value judgments and scientific facts. Regardless of an environmental impact statement's or other study's technical findings, many of the decisions to construct large-scale projects ultimately are made in the political arena and are based upon value judgments about the kind of society people want and the conditions under which they want to live. The public does not need a degree in science to hold and express deep convictions on the degree of risk or uncertainty it will accept in the building of a dam, a power plant, or a mass transit system or on how much it is willing to pay in benefits foregone or economic outlays in order to avoid or reduce that risk. This should always remain a subject of intense public scrutiny and debate.

Opportunity for public participation means more than a chance to react to a choice already made by someone else--a choice that citizens must pay for and live with. Because the public pays the bill, people are determined that the product they buy shall meet their needs. Citizens have a guaranteed right to explain their needs and desires throughout the planning and implementation processes and to have their views considered. Only on these terms will the public give its support. They are not so much interested in whether building a dam or mass transit system is feasible in engineering terms, but rather in why it is going to be built and in what it is going to do to them as well as for them. Therefore, the citizen's role also includes participation in the development of policy and formulation of alternatives. Too often no alternatives to con- struction projects are presented or even considered, except perhaps to debate how many dams or locks may be necessary to better accomplish the overall project.

What are the other alternatives for achieving improved management of our water resources or more efficient utilization of our energy sources? These should be posed to public meetings early in the planning process. Risk-benefit analy- sis is the technique generally used to weigh risks and benefits. It is not a technique, however, that yields precise and objective answers; rather, it is a framework for organizing available information. A sound analysis should present a full set of choices with appropriate data on cost, benefits, and hazards for each option and precise statements on the degree of uncertainty associated with each option. Even when these efforts are successful, the process still involves making trade-offs and sometimes comparing practical benefits with moral risks. Because this is so, risk-benefit analysis is highly subject to political pressure. Until some common denominator is dis- covered to bridge the gap between different value systems, if that is possible, it remains a rudimentary tool for judging safety and therefore belongs in the public decision-making arena where a variety of viewpoints can be accommodated.

It is up to you who have the knowledge and experience to accept the challenge to present the facts to citizens who will be affected soon enough and in such a way that they can make the necessary value judgments. It is much simpler to plan for people than to plan with them. The process by which the public makes value judgments is not a systematic one that can be computerized and subjected to mid-term correction. But the public's right to make those judgments is one that is basic to our political system, inefficient though it might be. As citizens receive more information, as their understanding broadens, and as they participate throughout the full course of planning and policy implementation, citizens will be able to move beyond their present crisis-oriented actions.

I. REGULATORY INTEREST

Prepared by Roger S. Boyd, Director
Division of Project Management
Office of Nuclear Reactor Regulation
U.S. Nuclear Regulatory Commission, Washington, D.C.

Practically everybody speaking thus far has had the opportunity to note that
it is, in fact, the regulators who really are the problem. In preparing the
interest summary report, which is supposed to cover all three workshops, I
realized that I know a lot about nuclear power regulation, a little about
water resources development regulation, and practically nothing about urban
and suburban mass transit regulation. However, the Washington Star immediately
came to my rescue: A major article was headed, "When it comes to Metro's
future, ask the federal government," and subheaded, "Bureaucratic delays slow
up transit projects." Quoting from the article: "The federal government is
tying up Metro projects with so much red tape that local officials feel they
are no longer in control of the transit agency's destiny. A month of simmer-
ing frustration with federal nitpicking boiled over at yesterday's Metro board
meeting with sharp criticism of the review policies of the federal Urban Mass
Transportation Administration." Then quoting a local politician: "A lot of
things they do cause delay and are based on just theories or conjecture."

After reading this, I figured that even as diverse as these workshops were
supposed to be, there was some indication that the same problems were sur-
facing, and I know that the perception of regulators was precisely the same.
In providing some summary remarks, I, therefore, will try to put the various
regulatory risk questions in four somewhat overlapping piles. I want to
speak a little bit about the risks from the point of view of the regulated--
not that that has not already been done because, of course, it has. I then,
of course, want to discuss the problems of the regulatory authorities themselves and to focus on where the problem areas come together. Finally I
want to discuss areas where some improvements might be made.

It seems that the principal sources of regulatory risk to the industry turn
out to be delay, uncertainty, and unpredictability. Delays are probably the
most costly and may be the easiest to attempt to quantify, but I think that
in fairness we all ought to look at delays in terms of additional time beyond
that originally conceived for some sort of regulatory approval. Many times I
see various facets of the industry talking about delay; they say: "It takes
two years to get a license and that is all delay." On the other hand, more
perceptive people will say: "If I know that it is going to take two years,
I will accommodate it; it is when it is going to take three or four years
that I have problems." I think uncertainty in the regulatory process and
unpredictability of regulatory requirements from time to time go hand in
glove to adversely affect industry decision making from the important
standpoints of time and money.

On the other hand, regulatory responsibilities are beset with their own tough problems. Those responsibilities, which in most cases are set down in appropriate laws, include consideration of what is and what is not in the public interest--health and safety and, certainly in the past few years, environmental protection. As a matter of fact, for nuclear regulation we have two more--common defense and security and antitrust. In my view, the problems of the regulators are both internal and external. Internally, it is very difficult to provide a precise enough regulatory envelope of require- ments and then be able to stay within it. Externally, it is correspondingly difficult for regulators to obtain on a timely basis the information they need to make these necessary regulatory decisions. I think the two problems combine to make it difficult and, in many cases, impossible for anyone, least of all the regulators, to be able to properly assess the impact value or cost- benefit of regulatory decisions.

I think these problems come together most vividly in the usual situation where there is an apparent need to involve many and overlapping jurisdictions-- federal, state, local, and, in the case of Metro, many locals. This has been mentioned a number of times, but what has not been brought out, and I believe it is true, is that this is probably just as much a problem for the regulators as it is for the regulated. In any event, it does contribute to a lack of effective decision making by all the parties involved. Probably also brought into the question is the shortcoming of adequacy and experience of all parties.

In presenting these summaries, we were supposed to identify and recommend new and improved policies that are needed, where they can now be initiated, and where research is required for their development and implementation. I wish I could do that; in fact, I wish any of us here could do that where the matter of regulation is concerned. The best I can do is to suggest some old ideas about areas where improvement might be made. First, there could be a greater specificity of regulatory requirements. On the other hand, this suggestion may be a good example of the cure being worse than the disease. Thus, it is some- thing that I would not jump into completely and instead would just urge us to be more specific.

I think all the organizations involved at the same time should strive to eliminate overlapping and redundant requirements. In some areas of regulation I am sure inroads are being made--probably not enough and probably not fast enough, but it is certainly something that should be encouraged and should be everybody's goal.

Early planning and early participation by all the parties also should be encouraged. A number of people have talked about the adversary nature of the various relationships and how bad that is. I am prepared to accept and agree with that, but a certain amount of it is probably inevitable. It is, perhaps, through early planning and early participation before the various construction projects get too far along that some of this adversary relation- ship may be ameliorated. It is clear that public hearings and court suits are adversary, and I suspect the chance of doing much there is very minimal. But in the general regulatory processes, it probably can be toned down somewhat.

The last thing I thought of is the use of standardized technology by the industry and by the corresponding regulatory agencies who would pre-approve the use of such standardized technology. This ought to go far to increase the efficiency and effectiveness of the regulation of these construction activities.

And after putting all this together, I decided to tie in a final thought, with which everybody here is entitled to either agree or disagree: I suspect that today's technology may well be too complex to attain these desired goals, to minimize the kinds of construction risks being discussed here today. But that notwithstanding, it is still clearly the goal for which we should all be striving.

Chapter V

PANEL DISCUSSION SUMMARIES

Five multi-interest panels were established and were charged with viewing the following critical problem areas identified from the standpoint of the interests involved, and, perhaps more importantly, in the context of the relationships among the parties to the construction process:

- Unknown site and market conditions
- Personal and organizational competence and performance
- Administration and management
- Allocation of risks and resolution of disputes under the contract and beyond the contract
- Insurance and bonding

Specifically, the panels were asked: (1) to identify steps that can be taken during the various phases of a construction project to avoid or to mitigate risks and equitably allocate responsibility for risks involved, and (2) to recommend actions that can be taken to improve relationships, practices, and procedures and, ultimately, will lead to reduced time and cost and improved performance.

In the first two panel discussions, emphasis was placed on the most critical risk factors identified during the workshops as identified by the Committee. For purposes of discussion, these were identified as relating to problems of "unknown conditions and personal and organizational competence and performance." In the three succeeding panels, emphasis was placed on practices, policies, and procedures currently employed during the construction process to deal with problems of risks and liabilities in construction that, at the same time, contribute to these problems. These were identified as relating to problems of "administration and management, resolution of disputes, and insurance and bonding."

Reports of each of the five panel discussions follow. Each includes remarks by the panel moderator and excerpts taken from the transcript of the discussion that reflect the critical problems and potential solutions identified by the panel. It will be noted that the same or similar concerns are expressed by the five planels because of the interrelationships and interdependency of activities and parties in the construction process. No attempt has been made to eliminate such repetition as it bears on the problem area under discussion in each case. Additionally, no attempt has been made to resolve differences of opinion; therefore, when they occurred, the differing points of view have been presented.

65

A. UNKNOWN SITE AND MARKET CONDITIONS

Moderator

John P. Gnaedinger, President, Soil Testing Services, Inc., Northbrook,
Illinois

Panelists

John T. O'Neill, Executive Officer and Chief Engineer, New York City Transit
Authority, Brooklyn, New York
Robert S. O'Neil, Senior Vice President, DeLeuw Cather Company, Washington,
D.C.
George A. Fox, Executive Vice President, Grow Tunneling Corporation,
New York, New York
J. Jack Hunkele, President, Foley Machinery Company, Piscataway, New Jersey
James Lapping, Director of Safety and Health, Building Trades Department,
AFL-CIO, Washington, D.C.
Charles Mathers, Vice President, Johnson & Higgins, New York, New York
Darrell McCrory, Partner, Monteleone & McCrory, Los Angeles, California
Desloge Brown, Chief, Inspections Branch, Division of Licensed Project,
Division of Bureau of Power, Federal Power Commission, Washington, D.C.

In its discussion, the panel concerned itself with risks involving site and
market conditions that are unknown or undetermined at the time of project
initiation. These included but were not limited to:

1. Unknown and changing geotechnical conditions of the site itself
2. Unpredictable natural hazards (such as earthquakes and floods)
3. Environmental hazards (such as job accidents, damage to existing
   structures, explosions, and disruption due to environmental,
   regulatory and citizens actions) and unknown and variable labor
   conditions
4. Economic risks (such as cost escalation due to inflation, availability of financing, and costs involved with delays in schedule)
5. Unknown and unforeseen market conditions (such as fluctuation in
   demand for construction facilities in general and for various
   types of structures in particular) and availability of materials
   and labor

In the discussion, the panelists considered the adequacy of site investigations,
the potential for predicting and for accommodating future economic conditions,
unexpected delays due to governmental regulations and administrative procedures,
personnel safety, and resource availability. Following are specific problems
and potential solutions identified by the panel.

1. Problems

    a. Unknown Site Conditions and Changed Conditions

        (1) Geotechnical and subsurface conditions present the greatest
        problem with respect to risks due to unknown site conditions,
        particularly in civil works construction involving under-
        ground construction. Intimately connected with the problem
        of unknown site conditions is the problem of differing site
        conditions that are bound to exist and the changed construc-
        tion conditions that can be expected to result. Clear recog-
        nition and equitable allocation of these risks often are not
        reflected in contract documents or in insurance coverage.

        (2) The contractor historically has been expected to assume the
        greatest portion of these risks. The owner or his engineer-
        ing consultant generally provides the contractor with infor-
        mation about geotechnical and subsurface conditions. The
        engineer typically determines what data are needed, and as
        the project matures from the preliminary planning to design,
        the knowledge of the ground becomes more complete. Additional
        borings are taken, studied, and analyzed. The engineer then
        presents the data in or with contract documents. The degree
        of disclosure presently ranges from a simple reproduction of
        the logs of borings to a complete geotechnical interpretation
        and report considering design and construction factors. The
        contractor then prepares his bid using the available data and
        his own experience and, in some cases, may hire an engineer-
        ing geologist or geotechnical engineer to make further inter-
        pretations. The owner then customarily selects the lowest
        bidder and awards the contract. Some of the realities of this
        practice are that it is virtually impossible for the engineer
        to have all the data necessary for complete knowledge of sub-
        surface conditions. The geotechnical data he collects normally
        are valid only at a given point, and the chance of identifying
        all discontinuities is very random. In urban areas, more geo-
        technical information and experience normally are available,
        but natural variations in conditions between borings still
        exist. On route type projects, borings may be made at 300-
        to 600-foot intervals, and it is questionable whether conditions
        can be predicted accurately between such point sources and data.
        Beyond supplying technical data, the engineer sometimes is
        hesitant to interpret the ground conditions because he feels
        that he is taking a liability that is not his to take. Further,
        in many cases, the boring program is oriented toward design only,
        instead of also considering the contractor's requirements.

(3) Unknown conditions regarding the location of existing utility and service systems and structures in urban areas present similar problems. Unless these systems and structures are properly identified and noted on drawings, they can present serious hazards and difficulties during construction.

(4) The contractor usually has only four to six weeks to analyze data and prepare his bid. In most cases, he is under pressure to present a low bid if he wants to be awarded the contract and, hence, he may be hesitant to take a pessimistic view of the ground conditions. In fact, a contractor who has particular information about poor ground may be at an extreme competitive disadvantage if he reflects this in his bid. Public agencies who must select the lowest bidder generally do not have the advantage of prequalifying contractors; they are required to seek a hard figure for budget and financial purposes.

(5) When changed conditions do occur, the contractural language often is unclear and changed-conditions clauses often are contradicted by exculpatory language protecting the owner's interest. The result is delays due to work stoppages and legal arguments as to which language takes precedence and general escalations in project time and costs. These problems are reputed to be less prevalent when dealing with some of the large federal agencies such as the Corps of Engineers and the Bureau of Reclamation that have long histories of dealing with civil works construction. However, state and local public agencies (e.g., water districts, city councils, and county boards) and the private engineering firms who draft their plans and specifications sometimes are unaware of the need for and effect of a changed-conditions clause in a contract.

b. Cost Escalation

(1) Cost escalation due to inflation and cost increases due to the numerous delays that can be encountered throughout the life of the project represent two of the most critical risks. No party to the process is immune to escalating costs. While the contractor normally bears 100 percent of cost escalation during project construction (the causes of which are beyond his control), ultimately it is the owner and the consumer who bear the final costs of all projects.

(2) Construction projects often require from two to six years or more to complete and many levels of government often are involved in financing and, thus, budget approval and allocation of funds. Disagreement regarding acceptable levels of inflation to be assumed often arise among the various jurisdictions (project authority and city, state and federal agencies) and the contractor who must make his own independent assumption.

69

c. Unexpected Delays Due to Governmental Regulation and Administrative Procedures

   (1) Governmental practices and procedures for dealing with admin-
        istration of funding responsibilities, approval processes,
        and environmental considerations, which involve all levels of
        government and the public in general, frequently result in a
        significant amount of delay on a project that cannot be predicted.

   (2) One area of greatest risk is the unknown delay or the possible
        cancellation of a project that results from environmental
        evaluations. There apparently is no clear limit placed on the
        actions of environmental objectors. Despite the careful pre-
        paration of environmental impact statements, their review by
        all believed to have interest in the project, adversary pro-
        ceedings conducted by regulatory bodies, the compilation of
        voluminous written records and evaluations and decisions
        rendered by regulatory agencies, the courts and, in some
        instances, the Congress seem to be the final arbitors.

   (3) Delays also can result because of the time-consuming process
        of securing permits, licenses, and approvals from a multiplicity
        of jurisdictions at federal, state, and local levels of govern-
        ment.

d. Personal Safety

   (1) Construction is inherently hazardous and accidents that result
        in personal injury and death are critical risks that can carry
        with them the heavy financial risks of project delay, third-
        party suits, and increased insurance costs. It was noted
        that ten times as much delay is caused by accidents as by
        strikes and other labor problems.*

   (2) Hazards can be designed inadvertently into the construction
        process by engineers who lack understanding of the processes,
        the work practices, and the equipment limitations generally
        involved in construction and particularly in construction
        of some innovative designs. Attention is given primarily to
        design calculation for the finished product, and loads and
        stresses encountered during construction, the analyses of which
        are assumed to be the responsibility of the contractor, may not
        be considered sufficiently.

---

*Cited by James Lapping, Director of Safety and Health, Building Trades
Department, AFL/CIO, Washington, D.C.

70

e. Materials and Labor Availability

    (1) Materials availability (with the possible exception of energy) and labor availability have not been serious problems in recent years (1974-77) due to the economic climate and depressed condition of the construction industry. However, when the labor and materials markets are tight, the risk generally is accepted solely by the contractor as a normal business risk and assumed under normal contingencies. Losses can result from delays caused by supplier, material and equipment shortages and labor shortages.

    (2) If a contractor fails to perform because of the unavailability of labor, only the owner can be compensated partially through the performance bond.

2. Potential Solutions

a. Unknown Site Conditions and Changed Site Conditions

    (1) All parties to the process should recognize that unknown site conditions are a reality, and an allowance should be made for the cost impact of these unknown conditions. It should further be recognized that this cost for changed conditions is a true project cost and does not represent an attempt to inflate the total cost to the owner.

    (2) The problem of unknown conditions should be dealt with first when plans and specifications are being drafted. The owner and the engineer have years to commission effective geotechnical studies, to take additional borings if required, and to analyze the results in terms of the design and construction. At the owner's request, an engineer should be retained to prepare a thorough geotechnical report that presents the basis for design. The owner should be briefed by the engineer when plans and specifications are being drafted as to what the various risks and liabilities are, and he should discuss in advance the risk of unknown conditions and how they might be dealt with in the contract so that all parties are aware of the responsibilities and liabilities that may occur due to potential changed conditions.

    (3) A site study including a thorough geotechnical analysis should be made available to all bidders. It is not reasonable to expect the contractor to analyze incomplete data in the bid period and quote a hard figure for the work. The owner also should recognize that a low bid in most cases does not represent the final construction cost. Additionally, during the design stage, designers and owners should consult with contractors to the extent practicable. Too often contract documents and the approach of the owners and the designers are

71

impractical because they do not reflect the realities of the contractor's work problems on the site. Implementation of the above practices should minimize the need for extra reimbursements to the contractor for changed conditions and should reduce job interruptions.

b. Cost Escalation

(1) A more equitable approach to the allocation of cost escalation due to inflation should be investigated in order to establish guidelines for escalation mechanisms to redistribute the risk on at least a shared basis. For example, an assumed index for escalation could be established and the contractor might be reimbursed on a percentage basis without overhead and profit for inflation beyond the assumed index.

(2) Guidelines for predicted escalation could be established by the federal government for use by both public and private owners. Appropriate agencies of the federal government (e.g., the Urban Mass Transit Authority) could develop guidelines to be applied by other jurisdictions that would include a base or index of what inflation might be expected as well as influencing factors that should be considered in arriving at assumptions at the local level. Such practice would provide a common basis for assumptions and justification of anticipated budgets and contract negotiation.

c. Unexpected Delays Due to Governmental Regulation and Administrative Procedures

(1) In an effort to reduce the disruption caused by protest once normal regulatory review actions have been taken, efforts to implement the National Environmental Protection Act should be reviewed. Congress and regulatory agencies also should avoid the retroactive application of new requirements to projects that have been previously authorized and are under construction simply because some new environmental concern is raised.

(2) Consideration should be given to the development of mechanisms for coordinating the responsibility for securing permits, licenses, and other approvals in order to reduce the delays that currently result because numerous parties to the process are dealing with a variety of governmental agencies at federal, state, and local levels.

d. Personal Safety

   (1) Accidents often are unavoidable; however, the conditions that
       present the hazards are not totally unpredictable and risk
       reduction through available preventative techniques can be
       accomplished. Hazard detection procedures that anticipate
       potential disruptive or dangerous events can be built into
       project scheduling and can reduce the risks. Construction
       hazard analysis utilizing trained safety engineers, project
       managers, union safety representatives, and staff also can be
       performed and can provide a format or structure for reducing
       or limiting the number of unpredictable events that cause
       accidents. When potential hazards are identified, expertise
       and experience can be directed towards improving those condi-
       tions with the highest potential for occurrence and for
       seriousness of injury, damage, or disruption.

e. Materials and Labor Availability

   (1) The depressed condition of the construction industry which
       has prevailed during recent years is not expected to continue.
       With increased construction activity, the energy shortage, and
       competing markets for resources that are becoming scarce could
       impact seriously on the construction industry. The adversary
       relationship among owners, engineers, contractors, material
       suppliers, and labor must be reduced if needs are to be foreseen.

   (2) Communication and cooperation among all the parties is essential
       in preplanning in order to anticipate material and labor demands
       well in advance of project execution and to be able to respond
       to crises that may arise.

73

B. PERSONAL AND ORGANIZATIONAL COMPETENCE AND PERFORMANCE

Moderator

Louis W. Riggs, President and Director, Tudor Engineering Company, San Francisco, California

Panelists

Donald A. Giampoli, Assistant Commissioner, Resource Development, Bureau of Reclamation, Department of the Interior, Washington, D.C.
Edgar E. Erlandson, Manager of Construction, Stone and Webster Engineering Corporation, Boston, Massachusetts
George T. McCoy, Senior Vice President, Guy F. Atkinson Co., San Francisco, California
Edward F. Delaney, Manager, Turbine Service Programs, Installation and Service Engineering, General Electric Company, Schenectady, New York
Charles Mathers, Vice President, Johnson and Higgins, New York, New York
W. Stell Huie, Partner, Huie, Ware, Sterne, Brown & Ide, Atlanta, Georgia
H. Allyn Parmenter, Training Department, United Association of Journeyman and Apprentices of the Plumbing and Pipe Fitting Industry, Washington, D.C.
Roger S. Boyd, Director, Division of Project Management, Office of Nuclear Reactor Regulation, U.S. Nuclear Regulatory Commission, Washington, D.C.
Celia Epting, Staff Specialist, League of Women Voters, Washington, D.C.

The risks associated with the particular subject of this panel, personal and organizational competence and performance, can be related to all activities in the construction process and apply to all parties in the process. Highlighted in remarks made in earlier conference summaries were problems having to do with selection of competent designers, qualifications of contractors, the quality and competence of those who adjudicate disputes, the knowledge and experience of regulators, and an informed public. Additionally, the panel discussion covered education and training, continuing professional development, licensing, organizational accreditation, quality assurance, quality control, and inspection. Indeed, problems and potential solutions associated with personal and organizational competence and performance will be found in all of the panel discussions. Critical problems identified by this panel deal with complexity and scale, adversarial relationships, responsibility and control, public action, procurement practices, and education and training. Following are specific problems and potential solutions identified by the panel.

1. Problems

    a. Complexity and Scale

        (1) The personal and organizational competence of all parties to the process are being affected seriously by the increasing demands and complexity of policies and procedures required in the regulation, administration, economics, and execution of large construction projects.

        (2) Many parts of the contract to construct are related to nonconstruction, socioeconomic considerations and place an administrative burden on the construction contractor beyond his primary responsibility to construct.

        (3) The increasing technological, economic, and sociological complexities of the construction process have created the need for many specialists beyond the classic management, design, construction, and labor expertise. Needed are knowledgeable people to handle programming; financing; computer technology; insurance; and legal, environmental, and social concerns.

        (4) The increasing need for specialization results in limited individual competencies that, in turn, result in increased fragmentation of responsibility, authority, and decision making. Lacking is the capability for forming a comprehensive overview that will permit the fragments of the many specialities to be coordinated and that will form a sound basis for judgment and timely decision making.

        (5) The duration of large construction projects, which can last seven to ten years, renders continuous staffing with competent personnel difficult. At the inception of the project, the tendency is to assign the most qualified, dynamic people; however, as the project ages, these "best" people are moved to higher levels of responsibility and their replacements often seem not to have comparable training, experience, perspective, and authority. If this condition progressively prevails within regulatory, owner, designer, and contractor organizations, the overall project performance suffers.

    b. Adversarial Relationships, Responsibility and Control

        (1) Because of the potential liabilities that may accrue to any interested party to the process, a great amount of time is expended to protect the various parties, detracting from the time spent in developing a better and more economical product. Procedural documents often are conflicting, ambiguous, and either general or all-encompassing. Contract and specification language, for example, is drafted to address all contingencies

76

without including the required specificity to meet problems when they arise, and an entire code can be referenced without definition of the specifics of the code which should apply. The needed specifics therefore are left to the individual to interpret and apply, but when serious conflict arises, the written word, albeit ambiguous, conflicting and nonspecific, takes precedent over personal competence.

(2) The personal and organizational competence and performance of each of the parties seriously affect the competence and performance of all of the other parties. For example, a competent person with commensurate authority may not be provided at the project level by the appropriate managements to negotiate and effect prompt dispute resolution so that the project can continue with minimum of disruption. All too often, the arbiters are the courts and issues are resolved remote from the project site and by individuals within the legal and judicial structure who are removed from and perhaps not expert in the technical and operational matters which led to the dispute.

(3) The contractor depends very heavily on the personal competence of the people whose roles occur earlier than his in the contract procedure--the owner's people, their financing plans, the way they handle environmental considerations and the necessary permits, how they go about obtaining the design of a project (with their own forces or with consultants), their assessment of probable cost of a project, whether they decide to take bids or negotiate a contract, the preparation of detailed plans and specifications and their clarity. Any inadequacies that exist in any of that work ultimately will reflect on the ability of the contractor to do his job and usually these inadequacies result in disputes.

(4) Recent studies performed for a private contractor indicate that a craftsman in executing his primary responsibility spends from 30 to 40 percent of the work day in actual hands-on labor and the remaining 60 to 70 percent, in indirect or nonproductive activity that includes waiting for instructions, waiting for equipment, and waiting for quality control inspection.*

(5) Added layers of control have affected the organizational competence of all parties--from owner to the labor force. On large construction projects, the size of the organizational structure involved has doubled or, in some cases, tripled. There is no evidence that larger organizations necessarily

---

*Based on work sampling studies made by Emerson Consultants, Inc., New York, New York.

produce better, higher quality products; however, there is
evidence that higher administration costs, longer time spans,
and communications and training problems do result with further
dilution of responsibility and higher risk exposure.

(6) Professional liability insurance covering designers and contractors
for the lack of competence and performance that results from
errors or omissions is practically unavailable, particularly
for larger firms, at a reasonable price and at deductible levels.

(7) Product liability insurance covering the performance of products
is almost as difficult to obtain as professional liability
coverage. Costs and deductibles involved have increased dramatically. One cause of this problem is considered to be the
judicially imposed, inequitable features of the tort recovery
law.

c. Public Action

(1) The general public has been advised of all manner of possible
shortcomings and risks that may be associated with large facility construction, and it now continually seeks further safeguards
through additions to regulatory restrictions, quality procedures, etc. Each layer of added requirements makes risk and
responsibility delineation more difficult.

(2) The competence and performance of the general public is
directly related to citizen education and participation.
Often the actions taken by some public action groups are not
based on such education and involvement of the public early
enough in the planning process and throughout project execution.

d. Procurement Practices

(1) Procedures currently practiced in the procurement of construction facilities are being questioned. For example, the
practice of competitive bidding to secure the lowest price
may not produce the most qualified contractor (or design
consultant) or, ultimately, the lowest cost. In addition to
sufficiency of price, the contractor's integrity, his competence on work of similar size and nature, his financial
strength, the extent and profitability of his other work,
his subcontractors, and his organization must be considered.

(2) Licensing of construction contractors has been suggested as
a means for ensuring qualified contractors; however, because
of the disparity of state licensing laws and control, this
practice is questioned. It also is viewed by some primarily
as a revenue-raising mechanism in many states.

78

e. Education and Training

(1) The experience of various industry representatives indicates
that many colleges and universities no longer prescribe the
opportunity to run tests and do other work that approximates
conditions encountered in the field, and graduating engineers
now have little or no practical experience. Absorbing this
mass of new professional talent and making it useful in the
field has been difficult for private industry. Some copora-
tions have initiated field engineering training programs to
equip field personnel with the kind of knowledge and background needed to function in a timely manner under field conditions, which today might involve legal action or other dispute
resolution, negotiating, understanding problems, and providing
necessary documentation of what has been done.

(2) The professional schools have only recently begun to include
job management in their curricula. Training individuals in
project management presents a tremendous opportunity for
effecting savings by controlling costs and meeting schedules
on major construction projects.

(3) It is important to recognize in the early stages of job training those individuals who are not qualified or not suited
for a particular job situation and to discourage them from
continuing so that incompetency and weakness will not be
perpetuated later in the process.

2. Potential Solutions

a. Complexity and Scale

(1) A more closely integrated control system that standardizes
such activities as drawing procedures, write-ups, and other
administrative tasks would improve overall organizational
performance.

(2) The contractor must have qualified and competent people to
perform specialized functions--realistic estimating, planning
of the job, engineering for plant set-up and equipment requirements (including a maintenance program for the equipment), conducting labor negotiations, insurance and bonding scheduling,
safety programming, negotiating financing and major purchasing
arrangements, payroll programming, timekeeping, and providing
legal services.

(3) Management of the contracting process requires a careful
assessment of the competence of people and the amount of
monitoring that must be done. The contractor must be careful
not to exceed his personnel resources by bidding excessively

and taking on additional work that cannot be competently handled. The factor that limits most contractors to the amount of work they can undertake is the number of people they have that are qualified to do the work.

(4) There is a need to concentrate on getting management personnel who have good common-sense judgment and decision-making ability and give them authority to coordinate the fragmented responsibility that results from the narrow-gauged specialization within the process.

(5) The competency of the management personnel of all project organizations should be analyzed so that weaknesses can be identified and strengthened throughout the life of the project.

b. Adversarial Relationships, Responsibility, and Control

(1) The owner, with his engineer, must clearly set forth the terms on which he expects the contractor to bid so that all bids will have the same basis and he can get the benefit of the lowest bid that is reasonable. The specifications must be comprehensive enough to assign the risks and to do so in an equitable way so that those who are assigned the risks can bear them.

(2) The adversary attitude must be overcome if reasonable settlement of disputes is to occur.

c. Public Action

(1) Many believe that the owner should be responsible for initiating and applying some type of citizen education process and for involving citizens in early stages of the planning process to help formulate policy and lay out alternatives that subsequently will be considered in public hearings. If citizens are informed at the outset of all the ramifications of a project, there should be a decrease in the need for redundant public hearings that repeatedly cover the same issues and that further serve to build up hostilities on all sides.

d. Education and Training

(1) Colleges and universities should give greater emphasis to courses that will train students in the circumstances that will be encountered in actual practice.

(2) Colleges and universities should give greater emphasis to project management as an important part of professional training.

(3) Management and labor should cooperate in the development of educational programs to improve the understanding and productivity of all personnel.

C. ADMINISTRATION AND MANAGEMENT

Moderator

Samuel L. Hack, Director, Office of Construction and Facility Management, U.S. Department of Energy, Washington, D.C.

Panelists

C. H. Sedam, Vice President, General Construction, Pacific Gas and Electric Company, San Francisco, California

David G. Hammond, Vice President, Daniel, Mann, Johnson & Mendenhal, Baltimore, Maryland

T. A. Nemzek, Senior Energy Advisor, J. A. Jones Construction Company, Charlotte, North Carolina

Edward F. Delaney, Manager, Turbine Service Programs, Installation and Service Engineering, General Electric Company, Schenectady, New York

Edward B. Howell, Jr., Risk Analysis and Research Corporation, San Francisco, California

M. G. Johnson, Counsel, Bechtel Power Corporation, Bechtel Corporation, San Francisco, California

John M. Parker, Director, Construction and Maintenance Department, International Brotherhood of Electrical Workers, Washington, D.C.

William Dickerson, Assistant Director, Office of Federal Activities for Resources Division Staff, Environmental Protection Agency, Washington, D.C.

Neal Potter, President, Metropolitan Washington Council of Governments, Rockville, Maryland

The key to the discussion of the panel on administration and management was the problem of organizing all parties so that construction projects could be planned and executed in a way that would avoid, minimize, or mitigate the consequences of the inherent risks. It was pointed out that solutions formulated to imitate the style and ideology of the rest of our technostructure would not and have not provided relief to the construction industry. The unique nature of the construction industry derives from the fact that each construction project is unique, and the creation of constructed facilities is more complex than the creation of most other products. Dedicated as the industry is to rationalize its efforts, it remains a labor-intensive industry where local production factors are extremely important and subject to extreme variation. The virtue of the industry remains its adaptability to meet changing demands and the variety of social purposes it serves, a virtue that should be exploited in finding solutions to the problems of the high degree of risks inherent in the process.

Considering the discussions at the workshops, delay in the orderly execution of a project appears to be the major risk to which management can look at for improvement. The critical problems identified by the panel dealt with preplanning, control, decision making, and team building; public awareness and communication; and governmental control. Following are specific problems and potential solutions identified by the panel.

1. Problems

    a. Preplanning, Control, Decision Making, and Team Building

    (1) The lack or ineffectiveness of preplanning, control, communication, and prompt decision making are major administration and management problems. These problems and the adversarial atmosphere that project participants experience derive from insufficient thoughtful attention being given to establishing realistic staffing, contract arrangements, organizational relationships, and operating procedures tailored to the magnitude and complexity of a particular job. The owner has the responsibility for assuring that project arrangements truly fit the task.

    (2) Failure on the part of management of all parties to provide for effective and timely decisions at any stage of the process can be critical. However, the decisions or lack of decisions made in the initial stages of the project can contribute significantly to the turmoil in what follows in terms of changes and resolutions and can cause delays and increase costs.

    (3) Structured and purposeful communication is essential if administration and management problems are to be avoided.

    (4) Teamwork is essential and adversary relationships are harmful; however, some managers believe that such relationships are necessary to maintain appropriate checks and balances.

    (5) Too often controls are viewed as negative or as intended to prevent some action rather than ("what the control juggernaut ought to be") as mechanisms for keeping the project on track in a safe, adequate, and timely manner. Controls should be geared to performance.

    (6) The owner or manager isolated from major project participants, either by protocol or by choice, frequently is surprised when a problem, unresolvable by others, comes to his attention long after its impact might have been alleviated by his input.

(7) If disputes are not expeditiously resolved, the need to repeatedly go back to focus on a situation soon becomes a problem in itself as individual memories tend to recast previous events toward self-protective interests.

(8) Efficient project administration involving documenting job events, billing, quality and safety assurance programs, OSHA reports, warehousing of equipment, maintenance of materials, and tracking physical and monetary progress is necessary to the smooth conduct of the business operation. These activities provide the job manager with information he needs to make intellegent decisions. The amount of documentation and paper work required is increasing dramatically. For example, about 3 million pages of documentation were involved among all of the parties in the construction of a nuclear power plant in 1965 while more than 20 million pages are required today.

b. Public Awareness and Communication

(1) One major reason an adversarial relationship prevails is that an atmosphere of distrust has built up among many people concerning the objectives and motivations of the total business community. This distrust has contributed to the establishment of stringent control activity. Also contributing to this negative climate is the lack of communication of need, true costs, alternative courses of action, and potential environmental, economic, and social impacts early in the planning process.

(2) Too frequently problems arise because the various outside impacts are not recognized. Managers may not be flexible enough to recognize that what appears to be the best solution may not be feasible given various constraints and may fail to accept alternate solutions that can be accomplished.

c. Governmental Control

(1) Legislation has given federal and state administrative agencies enormous power, but adequate staff has not been provided and they have not been made responsible for partaking in original decision making; nevertheless, these agencies have the power to override initial decision making at a later date after many millions of dollars may already have been expended on a particular project. It is difficult for federal agencies to deal with 50 states and many thousands of local jurisdictions with any degree of expertise. The legislative branches of government have placed responsibilities on agencies without providing the appropriations and the administrative machinery needed to handle these responsibilities.

85

(2) Procedures for implementing regulatory responsibilities may not be initiated early enough in the process, and once a project is well into the planning stage or, in some instances, into construction, actions taken as well as indecision by regulatory bodies and the public can cause serious delays and attendant loses.

(3) Mandates to regulatory agencies often are based on legislation that is general in nature, but the state of the art is such that implementation by the regulatory agencies and compliance by the construction industry is difficult because criteria and standards are lacking. For example, the National Environmental Protection Agency calls for identification and development of methods and procedures that will ensure that presently unquantified environmental amenities and values will be given appropriate consideration in decision making, along with economic and technical considerations. The state of the art is such that precise predictions of environmental impacts often cannot be made and much subjective judgment is exercised in the decision-making process.

(4) Coordination of responsibilities among regulatory agencies has been done on a piecemeal basis and has resulted in conflicts and delays as the various agencies carry out their responsibilities.

(5) Many recipients of federal grants must abide by a prior approval process wherein contracts, major change orders, supplemental agreements, and the like must be approved by the federal agency prior to proceeding. For example, the U.S. Department of Transportation tends to require that everything be processed through Washington for approval and it is hard to get the authority delegated out to the regional level. This can create delays to the owner and the contractor.

2. Potential Solutions

   a. Preplanning, Control, and Decision Making

   (1) Managers must balance risks and liabilities against the actions that are necessary for timely and efficient prosecution of large construction projects. To do this: (a) risks likely to be encountered in the specific project and situation must be identified initially; (b) experience, both good and bad, of how similar projects were handled should be reviewed in order to avoid similar failures but more importantly to take advantage of successes; (c) laws, practices, policies, and procedures that were previously used in the jurisdiction that governs the project should be reviewed; (d) to the extent possible, probable events or sources that might cause each type of risk should be identified; (e) the way and the

extent to which these risks will affect ability to efficiently perform planning, design, and actual implementation of the project should be assessed; (f) analysis should be made to determine how different project organizations might either alleviate or exacerbate the risks with particular attention to how to assign responsibilities and how to delegate authority so that a particular entity is able to meet the responsibilities efficiently; and (g) the amount and kind of controls that are likely to be exercised by other agencies and those that ought to be exercised by the manager himself should be assessed. Once the risks are identified and the method of management assessed, how best to organize the project should be determined, recognizing that there will be many outside influences that will impact on the project.

(2) Preplanning should be sufficiently definitive to determine contract arrangements that are best suited and sufficiently documented to make clear to all the early participants and those who come later what the requirements are with regard to responsibility, accountability, and flow of information. All major project participants should be a party to project planning at the outset and later in the project based upon the content of their project role rather than their contractual role.

(3) More thoughtful attention should be given to establishing more realistic staffing, contract arrangements, and operating procedures including allocation of authority for appropriate decision making at all levels of management and to tailoring them to the magnitude and complexity of a particular job.

(4) Credible and reasonable schedules must be developed and adhered to and required adjustments should be made expeditiously as work progresses.

(5) The construction industry should investigate the extent to which modern and advanced data processing techniques can be applied to increase the efficiency of construction activity administration.

(6) Labor should be considered a full member of the construction team and should be represented in the planning stage through prejob conferences and other means.

(7) In planning and executing construction projects (particularly those of long duration), consideration should be given to practical site conditions, such as providing for adequate access and the temporary facilities that are necessary during construction for the work force to perform its task effectively.

(8) The development by labor organizations at the national level of pattern or project agreements for use by local jurisdictions in collective bargaining agreements should be encouraged. Such pattern agreements should clearly spell out the responsibilities and rights of management with respect to labor. An example of such an agreement developed by the International Brotherhood of Electrical Workers follows:

> The union understands the employer is responsibile to perform work required by the owner. The employer shall therefore have no restrictions except those specifically provided for in the collective bargaining agreement in planning, directing and controlling the operation of all of this work, in deciding the number or kind of employees who properly perform the work, in hiring and laying off of employees, in transferring employees from job to job within the local union geographical jurisdiction, in determining the need and number, as well as the person who will act as foreman, in requiring all employees to observe the employer's and/or owner's rules and regulations not inconsistent with this agreement, in requiring all employees to observe all safety regulations and in discharging employees for proper cause.

(9) On large projects, a project control board or panel concerned with planning, control of participants in the project, communication, and decision making could be established. Membership would include key resident participants (i.e., owner, engineer, contractor, labor, and other major participants). The members would have defined authority from their respective organizations to settle project problems. The delegation of responsibility and authority would motivate the members to communicate fully, realistically, and in a timely manner and to develop the continuity of mutual understanding and knowledge needed to facilitate project decisions. For example, a project control board would review and approve changes and the sponsor of the change would be required to describe the change and its cost, its impact on other systems, and its impact on project cost and schedule and to demonstrate the need or the benefit. The arrangement should not affect the obvious rights of the owner but should introduce desirable discipline over changes. In addition, in the context of existing contract agreements, it could result in immediate determination of responsibility and would readily identify disputable items.

Such a board should meet frequently to review project status and should be prepared to cope with project problems as they arise. A reasonable, agreed-upon record of past group conclusions would maintain an atomosphere of credibility and reality throughout the life of the project and would mitigate the adversarial atmosphere that leads to a "no-winner" situation.

The structured communication that would result from a project control board could be the key to good management and administration and should be included in the project plan. Communication becomes progressively more important as project size and complexity increase and as unforeseeable problems become more likely. Involvement of the major participants would provide an objective test of the project planning function. A lack of preplanning would become more evident as the needs of each participant became more apparent. The group function would more effectively control participants in that a significant degree of self-control would be exercised as a natural consequence of membership on the board. Such an arrangement would improve performance of the management and administration.

b. Public Awareness

(1) Research is required to determine how best to structure and conduct an educational and communication program that will make the public aware of the risks and liabilities involved in and economic and social costs of major construction. Emphasis should be placed on identifying the audience for such a program and on developing mechanisms for reaching the right people.

(2) A reduction of the adversary relationship and better understanding on the part of the public is essential. One way of accomplishing this would be for the owners or initiators of major projects to hold a meeting(s) after a reasonable amount of planning had been done. (In some cases, sufficient preplanning may require the services of an architect-engineer.) Invited to this meeting should be representatives of leadership stature of each of the federal, state, and local regulating bodies (e.g., local air pollution control, water pollution control, forest service, fishing and game people); labor leaders, public representatives; and, possibly, recognized community leaders.

Those invited should be objective representatives who are open-minded and willing to consider all viewpoints, yet are adequately protective of the public interest. The purpose should not be to furnish a forum to those whose only dedication is to obstruct.

The agenda for the meeting should include a review of the need for the project, the options of what kinds of project can suffice, the options of location for the project, the demands of time, the costs to be expected, and, if possible, discussion of trade-off costs on some aspects of the alternatives. It would be of considerable help to have all these people together so that each can hear--and struggle with--the other's problems directly rather than hearing them through the owner. Thus, the meeting should be a forum for two-way communication to advise and receive advice, to learn the concerns of all parties, and to have each of the participants learn about the owner's views as well as those of other interests.

89

In the next stage of planning, an attempt could be made to meld all views into a plan. A follow-up meeting, or even a succession of meetings of the same parties, might be held to describe the results and receive reactions. Such an approach would not eliminate all conflicts but might give a broad base on which to restore credibility, to return regulation to an auditing function rather than a police function, and to meet the protests that ensue from those people who are dedicated only to obstruct.

c. Governmental Control

(1) The construction industry should actively provide input to regulatory agency planning processes that affect the industry and should be intimately familiar with the way agencies develop regulations so that it can provide advice with regard to regulations that are not reasonable with respect to implementation.

(2) In order to develop the new criteria, standards, and techniques needed to advance the state of the art and provide a sounder base for the development and implementation of regulatory requirements, research involving the private sector (and its practical experience) on a multidisciplinary multi-interest basis should be undertaken.

(3) The various regulatory agency responsibilities should be reviewed to identify conflicting and overlapping jurisdictions and requirements and to develop better regulatory administrative mechanisms that permit the construction industry to respond in a timely fashion.

(4) The federal government should recognize that local public agencies are governmental agencies and not private entrepreneurs. The federal government should share with the local governments the responsibility for funding research and development but should allow the local agencies to determine what should be studied and how it can be delivered. Such research and development should be directly related to the current needs of the industry and not directed solely toward new systems and concepts.

D. ALLOCATION OF RISKS AND RESOLUTION OF DISPUTES UNDER THE CONTRACT AND BEYOND THE CONTRACT

Moderator

John P. Buehler, Consultant, Bechtel Incorporated, San Francisco, California

Panelists

John Hoban, Deputy Director, Rail Transit Department, The Port Authority of
  New York and New Jersey, New York, New York
W. B. Schields, Vice President and General Manager, Gilbert/Commonwealth
  Associates, Jackson, Michigan
John Everson, Chairman, Parsons, Brinckerhoff, Quade & Douglas, San Francisco,
  California
William C. Cullen, Vice President, Johnson and Higgins, Washington, D.C.
Norman Burgoon, Jr., Executive Vice President, Fidelity & Deposit Company
  of Maryland, Baltimore, Maryland
Robert A. Rubin, Max E. Greenberg, Trayman, Cantor, Reiss & Blasky, New York,
  New York
John M. Parker, Director, Construction and Maintenance Department, Inter-
  national Brotherhood of Electrical Workers, Washington, D.C.

The major concerns of this discussion are those topics inherent in every project
regardless of size: contract provisions, contract administration, adequacy
of funding, change orders and their approval, and the resolution of disputes
within the contract terms and beyond. These subjects are relateable to the
layman and the professional as being part of the overall process. Entwined
with risk and liability are the key issues of selection procedures, schedules
for completion, bidding procedures, types of contracts, and availability of
bonding and insurance. The method and source of funding also impacts on the
risk question. Approvals are required prior to final financial commitment
but may not be one-time occurrences and often can extend down to individual
change orders. The motivation of the various parties involved also must be
examined, and who has the ultimate risk and what is likely to occur in the
event of a dispute must be considered.

As the drawer of the contract, the owner, and more often for the construction
and procurement contract, the owner and the engineer have available all the
words of the written language to express their intent clearly and without
ambiguity. Yet, when disputes arise in the course of or after construction,
all too often the position expressed by the owner is the written words did
not express exactly his intent. On the other hand, if a document is drawn
and includes, in the opinion of the bidder, inequitable allocations of
risk, the bidder should have reviewed the terms carefully and should not
later express consternation about those terms that he accepted or at least
acquiesced to in executing the contract. Contracts drawn for services in
the construction process of any project, particularly large complex projects,
should not reflect ambiguity as to intent.

Recognizing that the construction process is far from utopian, it is necessary to determine what can be done to develop new and improved relationships of policies, procedures, and practices that will reduce time and cost and improve performance by reducing the adversary climate and mitigating litigation.

Following are the specific critical problems and potential solutions identified by the panel that deal with contract conditions and contract administration, dispute resolution, and innovation.

1. Problems

   a. Contract Conditions and Contract Administration

      (1) In construction procurement, general contracting procedures are based on contracts of adhesion that are drawn by only one party and that cannot be changed in any way by the other party. These contracts are prepared by and for the owner and are highly detailed documents that too often limit in every conceivable way the owner's exposure to risks of whatever kind connected with performance of work under the contract and carefully assign those risks to the contractor and the engineer through exculpatory clauses (e.g., "hold harmless," "errors and omissions," and "field professional negligence").

      (2) The owner ultimately stands the greatest risks of all and these risks have become so traumatic that he has resorted to attempting to shift these risks to others by the production of "owner's contracts."

      (3) The engineer has little latitude or freedom of action in doing his job or in answering to his superiors. The contract documents that he is mandated to enforce permit him very little discretion. The engineer's remuneration generally contains no allowance for any consequential damages, hold-harmless clauses, patent infringements, or third-party suits.

      (4) Owners today, particularly government owners, generally do not have on the job a representative with full authority to settle disputes as they arise. In order to protect their own position, owners may prefer to have a court rule that frees them from possible blame or accusations that they may have made an erroneous settlement.

      (5) Contractors are accustomed to taking large risks. Faced with bad contract terms on a take-it-or-leave-it basis, on average size jobs, they add what they hope is a large enough contingency figure, hope the owner will be fair with them despite unfair contract terms, and submit a bid. But when unexpected under-ground or other conditions are found and owner-caused delays

develop or when other conditions occur over which they have no control, they hope the owner may be generous when the amount involved is manageable. However, on a $50, $100 or $150 million job, no public official can take the political or the fiscal risk of going beyond the contract terms where large sums are involved.

(6) There is no time during a four-week bidding period for the contractor to explore every public agency that might have an agreement with the owner. When these agreements turn up later, they have a great impact on the project and on the interpersonal relationships among the people who are involved in executing the work.

(7) The end date of the schedule of large projects often is preset and rightly so. Early delays are not recognized as critical; however, as the schedule becomes tighter, an attempt is made to compress the final completion of the engineering and construction contracts.

(8) While some believe that owner prequalification of contractors has some merit, others believe that the sureties are performing this function. The federal government recently asked the Government Accounting Office to make a study, which took about two years, of how the bonding operation was being handled on government work and of whether or not the government should do away with bonds and do its own prequalification. The study report reached a very definite conclusion that doing away with bonds would not be in the interest of the federal government.*

(9) Many contractors are staunch supporters of the competitive system of contracting; they believe that, as competent contractors, they are able to perform better for the owner and still at a competitive price. Some view with alarm negotiated contracts that open the door for political and other special arrangements to be made.

On some projects, the large dollar amount alone may alter the competitive picture. Some of these projects cannot be bonded and insurance availability is a serious question. In such instances, the firm price contract may not be appropriate.

On large projects, insurance interests report a higher frequency of claims on jobs that are competitively bid. It is believed by some that letting contracts only on the basis of bid price stimulates adversarial feeling, alienation, fragmentation, and breakdown in human relations.

---

*Cited by Norman Burgoon, Fidelity and Deposit Company of Maryland, Baltimore, Maryland.

(10)   Contracts often require equipment contractors to continue to
       carry all the risks until defects are corrected (e.g., in the
       case of railcar manufacturers, this can go on for two or three
       years); therefore, the contractor is required to continue carry-
       ing his insurance even though the owner also may be simulta-
       neously carrying insurance on the same risks. Everyone fears
       that if someone is killed when a car is in service, they all
       had better be protected. One manufacturer indicated that $100,000
       of the cost for a $600,000 car was for insurance. This duplicates
       coverage and increases cost.

(11)   In contract administration, losses occur because payments are
       not made promptly for work performed. Where federal grants are
       involved, the owner must wait to receive funds from the federal
       government and the contractor must wait to receive payment from
       the owner. Recipients of grants also are tied to a prior approval
       process wherein contracts, major change orders, supplemental
       agreements, and the like must be approved by the federal agency
       prior to proceeding. This can create serious and costly delays
       to the owner and the contractor.

       With regard to procurement of equipment, the owner wants to
       leave all payments until the end of the project, and the manu-
       facturer wants all the payments up front. If the owners provided
       for earlier payment, they would be partially relinqushing a means
       for ensuring satisfactory contractor performance.

b.   Dispute Resolution

(1)   The character of litigation in the construction industry has
       changed dramatically over the past 20 years. Traditionally,
       law suits were fairly clear cut and involved matters directly
       related to the construction process; suits by owners were
       relatively uncommon; the design professionals had to contend
       with virtually no litigation; and disputes were almost entirely
       confined to participants in the construction process.

       Today not only has the number of lawsuits dramatically increased
       but the nature of the lawsuits and the participants also have
       changed. Third forces, historically external to the process,
       today are the motivating factors behind a great many suits.
       These suits are not simply of the damage claim type where a
       plaintiff asks for money; rather, the whole litigation process
       adversely affects the business of getting projects completed.
       For example, in recent years mass confusion has been created
       in the nuclear licensing cycle by intervenors; while many of
       these intervenors are well intentioned, others are simply try-
       ing to defeat the whole concept of nuclear power without any
       particular concern for the merits of their case with respect
       to the particular nuclear plant that is going to be built.

94

In some of the larger lawsuits now pending by owners against engineers, contractors and suppliers, a more subtle external force--the regulatory commission--provides the motivation. In a number of states, a state public service commission or public utilities commission has forced a regulated company to proceed with lawsuits that it otherwise would not have filed. In one case,* a state public service commission formally advised a public utility that any further requests for rate increases would not be given favorable consideration until the utility filed suit against whoever was responsible for the problems being experienced with a particular power plant.

Again, 10 or 20 years ago, a lawsuit involving the construction industry was relatively simple from the lawyer's standpoint and developing the facts was generally not that difficult or time consuming and much less paperwork was involved. The main threat is not necessarily the dollar judgment that may be entered against a party to one of these cases since there may be a reasonable degree of assurance that ultimately justice will prevail and that any judgment either will be favorable or will reflect a reasonable dollar amount, except possibly in the case of bodily injury. Of more serious concern is the fact that far more money is spent in defending lawsuits than is ever awarded to any one or all of the parties. The cost of defense on one of these major complex construction lawsuits can literally run to hundreds of thousands of dollars per month. Simply allocating the risk among the parties more equitably by contractual or other means is not going to solve the problem unless a mechanism also can be established for resolving the disputes as they arise without the extremely expensive effort that now is necessary in any lawsuit.

(2) Arbitration has been suggested as one means of dispute resolution, but it does have some disadvantages because so much contemporary litigation involves people who are not themselves directly a part of the construction process. On a given project an owner can ensure that all his contracts with the engineer, with the contractor, and with the suppliers provide for some kind of arbitration process involving all the immediate parties to the project, but this will not account for all the people who become involved in lawsuits or who have information that is needed with respect to lawsuits. In a typical arbitration situation, one subpoenas the records of non-parties to get all the information that is needed. In a very complex dispute situation, arbitration as it stands today is not adequate.

---

*Cited by M. G. Johnson, Counsel, Bechtel Power Corporation, Bechtel Corporation, San Francisco, California.

(3) Perhaps some modifications of the despute-resolution system, such as the mediation-arbitration combination in which an attempt is made to resolve the problems as they occur, will solve some problems. Such a procedure, however, is not going to solve the problem that results in monstrous lawsuits which typically come into existence only after the facility is completed, operations commence, the facility does not operate as the owner or as the public thought it was going to, and someone's expectations are not fulfilled.

(4) It is usually in one party's interest to delay the resolution of a dispute for a period of time (e.g., the party has the use of money for a longer period of time or, perhaps more importantly, has more leverage when settlement negotiations are under way).

Slowness becomes institutionalized and the party paying out the money has nothing to gain by being expeditious. Also, the resident engineer or the contracting officer can be subject to criticism if he resolves disputes quickly, particularly in light of exculpatory clauses. Frustration results when the contractor has spent the money and is waiting for the dispute to be resolved while the contracting officer or the resident engineer does not have it in his power, or does not see it as his job, to resolve the dispute quickly. This could be at the very heart of the adversary relationship that develops.

(5) With regard to cost of litigation, the U.S. legal system is completely different from the British and European systems which provide for attorney's fees to be paid to the successful party. The June 1977 issue of the <u>American Bar Association Journal</u> notes:

> The general American rule is inequitable and jurisprudentially dysfunctional because it not only results in truncated justice in most cases, but also deprives the legal system of important leverage to induce settlements, and thereby reduce the volume of litigation. Its natural tendency is also to discourage pursuit of legal remedies in support of valid claims and defenses when the price of doing so is unaffordable or renders the remedy uneconomical, and to encourage the assertion of spurious, although culpable, claims and defenses to induce settlements for less than what it would cost the other party to litigate.

c. Innovation

(1) The risk of serious disputes often arises when technical specifications are innovative (e.g., when innovative major equipment is not introduced through the research and development process where provision is made for the new concept or

96

design to be fully tested). When innovation is made part of
the production contract, there is pressure to reduce testing
of early production units in order to meet publically stated
service commitments. Lacking accepted industry criteria and
standards, the owner must rely completely on the proprietary
information provided by the initiator. This situation occurred
with rapid transit cars when new owners were entering the field
and spurring innovation; with the mix of new owners, new designs,
and new manufacturers, serious problems arose that resulted in
major contract disputes as well as car prices that increased
at a rate far beyond the inflation rate for the rest of the
economy.

If the manufacturer is required to provide a fully built and
tested prototype before entering production, he experiences a
long delay between the fabrication of the prototype and the
tooling up for production runs. During this protracted period,
sources of supply for some of the parts may change, which could
have an adverse effect on the production model. Additionally,
if the owner commits himself to a proprietary product, he may
be faced with higher cost due to lack of competition and being
a potential captive of a single producer.

2. Potential Solutions

a. Contract Conditions and Contract Administration

(1) Contract language must be improved to more clearly, more
explicitly, and more fairly allocate risks.

(2) Risks to be borne by the parties must be clearly defined and
assigned in the contract. The risks should be borne by a party
able to control the risk before the event or, in the case of
unknown conditions, by a party able to shoulder the undefined
risk afterward.

(3) Plans and specifications should display or at least reference
all interagency agreements that will affect the course of the
construction project.

(4) The contract should clearly define procedures that assign
responsibility and authority for dealing with risks in a
specified time so that disputes are not allowed to escalate
over a period of months and even years and require final
ajudication in the courts.

(5) The owner should not try to relieve himself of the responsibility
for the adequacy of subsurface information that is obtained for
the purpose of the contract and furnished to the bidder; however,
it may be appropriate to identify information, opinions, and
interpretations obtained from others.

97

(6) In most cases, procedures can be instituted to regulate or control changes so that any change which is arbitrary or which is done on behalf of the designer or the owner is fully documented and is agreed to by the owner.

(7) In contract negotiation, the engineer should clearly recognize the distinction between the practice of his profession to a customary, professional standard of care and a commercial business risk. The engineer should recognize that he is not flawless. He should recognize that the established cost of engineering is based on services he is expected to perform as an engineer and that they do not include any amount for risks beyond those inherent in exercising only professional, customary standards of care. He should accept responsibility to furnish only services that can be defined at the time of negotiation since the normal engineering fee does not provide any contingency for undefined risks.

(8) On large projects, an alternative to competitive bidding is a target price contract.

(9) An experienced and strong resident engineer with responsibility and authority should be provided to deal with the contractor in the field. With reasonable checks and balances and audit, he should have some authority to spend reasonable amounts of money or at least to commit these subject to a later check. If this is done, he and the contractor can work out emergency situations and will not have to wait for months during which the situation becomes worse with litigation resulting. Such an individual, if sensitive, also can eliminate or reduce the possibility of disputes arising from public activities that are outside or beyond the contract.

(10) Better procedures should be developed for timely payment for work performed. When the federal government procures services directly from a contractor, it has the ability to establish a line of credit on which the contractor may quickly draw payment in his locality.* (For example, the MARTA project in Atlanta has secured agreement in principle to utilize this procedure. The federal government will audit the system that the MARTA project uses to control costs and schedule and, if it is found satisfactory, the delays and expense associated with the prior approval process can be minimized.)

(11) A more equitable approach to progress payments to manufacturers of major equipment is needed so that their cost can be reimbursed substantially as the equipment passes through the fabrication

---

*Treasury Circular 1075, third revision.

process, thereby reducing finance cost and encouraging prompt progress on the job. Better benchmarks for progress payments should be developed.

(12) Perhaps, instead of using payment to ensure contract compliance, the owner should have the right to insist that certain key contractor personnel be designated and given the responsibility to work on the contract and ensure compliance.

b. Dispute Resolution

(1) Vehicles should be developed for settling disputes quickly at the job site so that impartial resolution can be achieved promptly.

(2) Appropriate contract clauses and legislation can be used to provide incentives for speedy resolution of disputes, such as the imposition of interest paid as a cost of the contractor's rate of borrowing money or payment of the successful parties attorneys fees and the cost of preparing or defending against the lawsuit.

(3) A possible alternate form of dispute resolution might be the formation of "a center for the resolution of construction disputes," funded perhaps by a small percentage of construction contracts (e.g., the way union, welfare, and pension funds are financed). Such a center would be in a position to develop and perfect new and improved methods for resolving construction disputes (e.g., arbitration where there are consecutive hearings before a panel of specially selected, highly qualified arbitrators).

(4) Another possible form of dispute resolution is the process known as mediation-arbitration (med-arb) in which an individual or panel is appointed to serve as mediator to attempt to resolve a dispute in the first instance and, if that is not possible, to act as final binding arbitrator.

(5) When jurisdictional disputes are involved, greater use should be made of the procedures followed by the National Joint Board for Settlement of Jurisdictional Disputes. The Board has evolved into an impartial dispute group with a full-time chairman and part-time members. There is an appeals board and also provision for a hearings panel. Hearings are held every week. A case is referred by the Union or a contractor and five days are allowed for parties to assemble information on the case. Decisions apply only to the particular job in question. Work cannot be stopped and the parties must abide by the assignment made, which cannot be changed. Cases usually are processed within two weeks.

99

(6) With regard to the competence of judges, it is unrealistic to
     expect judges who deal with criminal, automobile, and matrimonial
     cases to be able to come to grips adequately with construction
     cases that require an understanding of so much underlying technology.
     Chief Justice Burger of the U.S. Supreme Court recently acknowledged
     the inadequacy of the courts in dealing with specialized problems
     and encouraged the formation of alternate forms of dispute resolution.*

c. Innovation

   (1) In the matter of innovative technology and new methods and
        equipment, risk factors should be shared by all parties. The
        contract language should provide for a thorough understanding
        with the owner of what the risk factors are and of what the
        limitations of risk to be borne by the parties are.

   (2) Research is needed on how to deliver new concepts into the market
        on a competitive basis and at the same time provide for the
        required safeguards for public safety and appropriate performance.

---
*Cited by Robert Rubin, Partner, Max E. Greenberg, Trayman, Cantor, Reiss
and Blasky, New York, New York.

E. INSURANCE AND BONDING

Moderator

David G. Hammond, Vice President, Daniel, Mann, Johnson & Mendenhal,
Baltimore, Maryland

Panelists

C. H. Sedam, Vice President, General Construction, Pacific Gas & Electric
Company, San Francisco, California
Dwight Glascock, Vice President and General Manager, Hydro and Water Resource
Division, Charles T. Main, Inc., Boston, Massachusetts
George T. McCoy, Senior Vice President, Guy F. Atkinson Company, San Francisco,
California
Norman Burgoon, Jr., Executive Vice President, Fidelity and Deposit Company,
of Maryland, Baltimore, Maryland
M. G. Johnson, Counsel, Bechtel Power Corporation, Bechtel Corporation,
San Francisco, California
Lawrence McReynolds, Stokes and Shapiro, Atlanta, Georgia
Edward B. Howell, Jr., Risk Analysis and Research Corporation, San Francisco,
California

Insurance and bonding traditionally have been the principal means for handling
risks and liabilities in the construction industry. However, in identifying
the problems associated with insurance and bonding in the construction industry
today, the panelists recognized that costs of insurance and claims settlement
are skyrocketing, markets (capacity) for insurance coverage are shrinking due
in large part to heavy insurance losses, and the insurance industry finds
coverage of construction projects unattractive (particularly those located in
urban areas where claims are likely to be larger). The failure of many to
recognize that it is impossible to cover all risks with insurance and the still
general use of inequitable allocations of risks and of unfair contract terms
are the issues underlying these problems.

1. Problems

    a. Insurance

        (1) Insurance costs have escalated as have other construction costs
            to the point at which insurance is practically unavailable in
            some instances.

        (2) The total value of insurance premiums paid by U.S. business in
            1975 (the last year for which data are available) was $25 billion

and it is probably twice that today or of the same magnitude as total corporate profits and that of corporate taxes in the United States.*

(3)   In 1975, the insurance industry had an underwriting loss of $4.9 billion; during 1976, the loss was $2.23 billion and in the first quarter of 1977, it was $543 million.**

(4)   Insurance for large construction projects is particularly unattractive to the insurance industry because many of these projects are located in highly urbanized areas where the slightest amount of damage is likely to result in enormous claims. In addition, most of the claims have involved what insurers term a "long tail" or "a long maturation period" (i.e., damage may occur today but claims and settlements will not occur for five or even ten years or more and the results will not be known for a long time). Given the kind of financial constraints that currently exist, insurance companies find such construction projects very unattractive.

(5)   Eighty percent of the dollar loss paid by one insurance underwriter is attributable to defense and claims attorneys' fees and costs (e.g., on a recent $2 million claim, $1.7 million went to the lawyers on both sides of the controversy).***

(6)   It is impossible to obtain complete coverage for any particular risk. The greatest risks encountered by engineers for which they seek insurance coverage are human error, consequential damages, hold-harmless provisions for others, third-party suits initiated on the "deep-pocket" theory, and patent infringement indemnity. Of these, human error presents the greatest problem. This risk also is the only one the engineer has major control over because errors come about as a result of his design and specification work. Consequential damages, hold-harmless provisions, third-party suits, and patent infringements are more affected by others than by the engineer himself.

(7)   Among the risks for which the contractor insures himself (beyond those for employee coverage) are builder's risk, third-party liability, and equipment. These coverages have become extremely

---

*Cited by George McCoy, Senior Vice President, Guy F. Atkinson Company, San Francisco, California.

**The National Underwriter, A. M. Best Company, Best Insurance Reports, Oldwick, New Jersey.

***Design Professional Insurance Company, San Francisco, California.

expensive and are not readily available. Recent judgments have forced the costs of these types of insurance to rise dramatically.

(8) Self insurance is appropriate for minor risks such as equipment insurance, but it is not realistic for liability coverage.

(9) While construction and product liability policies are made on a current basis, most of the professional liability policies are made on a "claims made" basis and a claim arising from a project five or ten years ago is covered by a policy in effect at the present time. If a professional engineer cannot find insurance coverage as claims arise, he and his assets are at the mercy of the courts.

(10) There is some disagreement, usually where there is a vested interest, regarding owner-controlled or wrap-up insurance. In wrap-up insurance, one party, usually the owner, provides at least third-party liability insurance for the various participants in the construction process. Typically, workman's compensation and builder's risk also may be included in the package.

Several recent studies indicate that wrap-up insurance seems to have many more advantages over conventional insurance, particularly in reduced cost and market availability. On jumbo contracts involving hundreds or even thousands of prime contractors, subcontractors and sub-subcontractors, the underwriting capacity of the world insurance community is just not large enough to provide all the necessary policies and amounts of coverage for all the contractors involved, thus leaving wrap-up as the only sensible solution if the project is to be insured.

On the other hand, it is argued that wrap-up insurance does not really make that much sense if all or most of the work is being performed by a single contractor. Wrap-up insurance may be desirable when a number of contractors are involved on a large project and the project involves some reasonably hazardous work posing a number of risks. Wrap-up insurance is appropriate only when adequate coverage really can be obtained and not just promised at the outset. Many wrap-up programs fall far short of what is intended at the outset in terms of the quality of the coverage, particularly if the engineer is to be covered. Almost without exception, they will not cover pure errors and omissions (i.e., damage that does not involve physical loss or damage). Some policies will pick up the bodily injury and property damage flowing out of the professional services although even those are fairly hard to get these days.

Another disadvantage is that at the outset of a project owners are unaware of how long it will take to get the wrap-up policy into effect. As a result, there are no specific insurance terms when the first contracts or subcontracts are awarded. The contractor then either must provide his own insurance or the risk must be taken by trying to paraphrase what the wrap-up program is going to be, which itself is a high-risk activity. The wrap-up program certainly can contribute to delay at the outset of the subcontracting process.

The wrap-up policy also can be a source of delay during the performance of the work. When a contractor is working under his own insurance, he presumably knows the things for which he is covered. If he is working under somebody else's insurance, he is not sure of what the exclusions are or of what they may mean. For example, under his own insurance he knows the limitations and what he may have to do. With wrap-up insurance, he may find that he has to stop his operation in the field and get the client's insurance administrator to determine what is and what is not covered.

A serious problem for everybody that is insured is the relative disinterest of wrap-up insurance. The insurer is not seeking a long-term relationship with each of the insurees. As a result, the interpretation and administration of the wrap-up policy tends to be very formalistic and legalistic. When one is dealing with a wrap-up insurance program, the insured do not have a long-term relationship or rapport with the carrier, and the carrier has no real incentive to treat them equitably; instead, he will treat them in a legalistic fashion. The shared limit can be a problem; if the owner is providing $25 million coverage, that limit may be shared with every other insured on the project. Also, if the annual aggregate limits of liability are specified, one might find that by the time his misfortune occurs the policy limits have been fairly well exhausted by other contractors.

A clear disadvantage from the owner's standpoint is cost. However, it is difficult to tell at the end of a job what the insurance actually cost.

The lack of long-range commitment by the insurors creates the tendency for the coverage to disappear during the course of a project. Unfortunately, particularly in the case of professional liability, the engineer does not really have much risk exposure during the course of the project, even with straight property damage and third-party property damage coverage. A contractor typically is looking to a wrap-up program for coverage of completed operations. If 75 or 90 percent of the way through a project, the owner's wrap-up program is cancelled before completion (where the program is not written for the life of the project with a "no cancellation" clause), the owner may instruct the contractor to provide his own coverage for which he will be reimbursed. The contractor could have a problem finding an alternate insurer willing to assume all of the risks of the completed operations period still ahead. For these reasons, wrap-up programs need to be given more thought than they have received. They are proper in some situations, but they are not the answer to all problems.

(11) With regard to power plant construction, an effective procedure for handling the fire protection recommendations of Nuclear Regulatory Commission and Nuclear Insurance Pool at an early stage in project designs is needed.

b. Bonding

(1) Surety companies are just emerging from three years of very serious losses on construction bonds, losses far greater than at any time since the Great Depression.

(2) The surety, under its bonds, guarantees to the project owner that the contractor will complete the job on time for the agreed price, follow the contract terms faithfully, and pay all the bills for labor, material, and subcontractors. Because a surety must make good if the contractor fails, whatever risk factors impact on the contractor concerns the surety with equal force.

(3) The risk factors that are of most concern to sureties are size, time, payment delays on change orders, and contract terms and conditions. The trend, particularly on water resource and power plant projects, is to package in a single construction contract many diverse sections that formerly were awarded incrementally. Some feel that this packaging affects some economies in time, supervision, and cost; however, there are several disadvantages that impact contractors, sureties, and the owners alike. There are more and more single, fixed-price proposals of $150-, $200-, $250- or even $400-million, and some run six or seven years. Contractors normally form joint ventures for such huge, long-term jobs in order to spread out the tremendous financial risks of labor and material increases, strikes, mistakes in judgment, fluctuating interest costs, and natural calamities that they cannot insure. Also, joint ventures often are needed on such big projects to provide the working and risk capital to qualify for suretyship. Even so, the sureties' capacity is being tested and their appetites are lessened for these huge exposures on long-term jobs, particularly when the contract terms are onerous and unfair. Sureties are increasingly concerned and cautious about their exposures on bonds covering multi-million dollar, long-term heavy engineering contracts, and the effective capacity of the surety market has been eroded. Owners, too, may

be mistaken in their reasons for packaging five-, six-, or seven-year projects into one fixed-price "jumbo" contract. One need only consider the huge contingency dollars that must be added by the contractor and the tremendous problems, delays, and costs, that flow from a possible default.

Of special concern are payments for change orders. Increasingly it seems that contracts are being rushed into the award stage before all the customary design work is completed. While this gets the project under way sooner, it multiplies the number of change orders that must be made as the work progresses. The extra work is ordered, but in far too many situations the final pricing of the extra work is not agreed upon for many months; in the meantime, the contractor receives no money, his cash gets short, his bills may go unpaid, his ability to take on new work is jeopardized, and the potential for default is increased.

Among the risk factors involved in the activities of sureties, none is more important or serious than unduly onerous and unfair contract terms. Historically, construction contract terms have been drafted by the owner without input from the contractors. (Often, the federal government is an exception; however, this is certainly true of other public and private owners that award a large percentage of the heavy engineering contracts in the country.) Many private and public owners impose liability on the contractor for owner negligence, engineering mistakes, or even for injury to third parties by reason of the contractor's just having assumed the job.

The owner does not always prevail in unfair contract terms, but he often does. Sometimes a contractor goes bankrupt or ends up in a four- or five-year lawsuit and, in the meantime, is badly damaged. In one currently pending case, the contractors have lost over $100 million of their own money; the job has been stopped and will be delayed for several years, which will increase costs astronomically; and litigation is going to take years and cost millions.*

(4) It has been suggested that environmental intervenors be required to give surety bonds to prevent them from further delaying a job once a decision has been reached by the courts. Token bonds, however, would not be adequate to cover the vast losses that are caused by further delay. According to surety interests, bonds in amounts that do any good just cannot be obtained for this purpose; there would be no market for them. None of the agencies or the environmentalists would have the funds to justify such a surety bond; therefore, it is not a viable alternative to the problem.

---

*Cited by Norman Burgoon, Jr., Executive Vice President, Fidelity and Deposit Company of Maryland, Baltimore, Maryland.

(5) The present 100 percent bond requirement is redundant. It is not required by federal law, contrary to what is commonly believed, and it unnecessarily restricts the surety market's ability to respond in a proper way on these big jobs.

(6) In connection with the Small Business Administration bond program, there are proposals in several states to create assigned risk pools for handling marginal contract bond business. It is felt that the easy access to bonds hurts the qualified contracting industry. Further, it is felt that the program encourages emerging contractors to undertake obligations for which they are not capable and do not have prior experience and could result in the contractor's bankruptcy. The sureties are not interested in participating in these assigned risk pools.

2. Potential Solutions

a. Insurance

(1) Measures can be taken that would reduce insurance costs dramatically. Hold-harmless and indemnity clauses should be eliminated from construction contracts. They may cost an owner as much as 0.5 percent of the total construction cost, and the benefit they give him is miniscule. Ultimately, the people who have agreed to hold someone harmless will have an insurance company that will fight them, and the courts usually will say those agreements were gained under disparate bargaining power and will not allow them to shed their liability. If such clauses were eliminated, cost of insurance would go down.

(2) Because the insurance industry is not going to readily respond to the problems of the construction industry, creativity is required and there are techniques for reducing cost that have not yet been used by large owners of projects. One of these would be to consider spreading the risk over a chronological period of years rather than among members of the construction process. The construction period should not necessarily bear all of the cost by itself of the enormous risks that occur during that period. The risk should be spread, just as is the cost of the materials, over the life of the project. It would be possible to chronologically stabilize insurance costs over a protracted period of time. This technique has been used with distressed insurance situations and has worked well for foundation engineers in private practice who could not buy insurance.

(3) Wrap-up insurance can be good for some projects and bad for others. Each project has to be examined and, based upon the factors involved, a decision made by the owner as to whether wrap-up insurance should be used. Owners in general should recognize that the risks connected with construction ultimately

are theirs and that they probably should be paying the entire cost of the insurance, which would eliminate the duplications that occur. Wrap-up does this in essence. However, there could be a conflict in the professional liability area. Professional liability insurance has made engineers and architects targets, and it may be in the financial interest of owners to forgive professional liability that is not the result of wanton or culpable behavior. To hold a professional man liable for acts of simple negligence is not using good fiscal sense.

(4) The innovative concept of risk management is offered by some as a solution to the problem of cost and availability of insurance. This concept requires the owner to firmly take control and to determine his risk and loss potential and develop an appropriate program. The risk management process requires: (a) identification and analysis of risk of accidental loss; (b) the development of methods of treating risk; (c) the selection of the best method for coping with the risk; (d) the implementation of the best method; and (e) monitoring the results to make adjustments if necessary.

Once the owner has processed his risk, the specific techniques of risk management may be utilized; these are avoidance, retention, prevention, and transfer. Insurance professionals agree that utilization of risk management principles by owners and the incorporation of such principles into the design of projects will significantly reduce some of the pressures on the insurance market and will decrease the cost of insurance.

(5) Insurance companies should provide more professional assistance to the insured in accounting and safety programs and risk analyses in order to minimize or eliminate risks and reduce costs. Small organizations have very limited assets and may not have adequate personnel to handle prolonged and difficult litigation.

(6) Insurance-related engineering personnel should work with owners and with designers' buyer protection personnel so that early consideration can be given to insurance-related fire protection items.

b. Bonding

(1) Awarding authorities should recognize that the packaging of multifaceted projects into single fixed-price contracts of several hundred million dollars that continue for five, six, or seven years is not advantageous to the contractors, the sureties, or the owners.

(2) The impact of increasingly large contracts would be eased by lowering the performance bond requirement to 50 percent of

the contract price. The Office of Management and Budget and Environmental Protection Agency will approve such reductions only on a case-by-case basis.

(3) Long-term contract problems could be alleviated by more reasonable contract conditions and by inclusion of escalation provisions for increases in labor and material costs.

(4) Architects and engineers can and should help to influence the owners to write fair terms. Many times in the past designers have contributed to the problem by feeling that they are the owner's agent, and they can help him by passing on all the obligations to the contractor.

(5) Surety companies should provide greater assistance to the contractor regarding default to make the project flow easier and to avoid litigations.

(6) Contractors and surety groups need to work actively with owners' representatives before plans and specifications are drawn.

APPENDIX A

WORKSHOP PARTICIPANTS
AND
PROJECT DESCRIPTIONS

URBAN AND SUBURBAN MASS TRANSIT CONSTRUCTION WORKSHOP
JANUARY 18-19, 1977

CHAIRMAN

B. R. Stokes, Executive Director, American Public Transit Association,
Washington, D.C.

PARTICIPANTS

Owners

William D. Alexander, Assistant General Manager, Transit Systems Division,
    Atlanta Rapid Transit Authority, Atlanta, Georgia
Roy T. Dodge, Chief, Design and Construction, Washington Metropolitan
    Transit Authority, Washington, D.C.
John Hoban, Deputy Director, Rail Transit Department, The Port Authority of
    New York and New Jersey, New York, New York
John T. O'Neill, Executive Officer for Construction Administration and Chief
    Engineer, New York City Transit Authority, New York, New York

Designers

James A. Caywood, Senior Vice President and Director, DeLeuw, Cather & Company,
    Washington, D.C.
Paul E. Conrad, Executive Vice President, Wilbur Smith & Associates, Columbia,
    South Carolina
John E. Everson, Chairman, Parsons, Brinckerhoff, Quade & Douglas, Inc.,
    San Francisco, California
David G. Hammond, Vice President, Daniel, Mann, Johnson & Mendenhall, Baltimore,
    Maryland
E. E. Wilhoyt, Jr., Project Manager, Bechtel Associates Professionals Corporation,
    Washington, D.C.

Contractors

C. H. Atherton, Vice President and Area Manager, J. F. Shea Company, Inc.,
    Bethesda, Maryland
George A. Fox, Executive Vice President, Grow-Tunneling Corporation, New York,
    New York
Richard E. Hall, President, Underground Construction Company, Inc., San Leandro,
    California
George J. Tamaro, Vice President and Chief Engineer, ICOS Corporation of America,
    New York, New York

Manufacturers and Suppliers

J. Jack Hunkele, President, Foley Machinery Company, Piscataway, New Jersey
A. G. Maier, Manager, Mass Transit Sales, General Railway Signal Company,
New York, New York

Labor

Allan Burch, Director of Safety, International Union of Operating Engineers,
Washington, D.C.
Joe M. Short, Director, Education and Training, Laborers' International Union,
Washington, D.C.

Insurance

William C. Cullen, Vice President, Johnson & Higgins, Washington, D.C.
Hiram L. Kennicott, Jr., Vice President and Manager of Commercial Lines Under-
writing, Kemper Insurance Companies, Chicago, Illinois
V. Wallace Ryland, President, Fred S. James Company of Virginia, Arlington,
Virginia

Legal

W. Stell Huie, Partner, Huie, Ware, Sterne, Brown & Ide, Atlanta, Georgia
Larry S. McReynolds, Partner, Stokes & Shapiro, Atlanta, Georgia

Public Awareness

Neal Potter, President, Metropolitan Washington Council of Governments,
Rockville, Maryland

URBAN AND SUBURBAN RAPID TRANSIT PROJECT DESCRIPTION

The project is an extensive, new rail rapid transit system (50 to 100 miles)
serving a major urban area and its surrounding suburbs (2 to 3 million people).
It is being designed and constructed under the authority and direction of an
especially established authority over an extended period (8 to 12 years) at a
substantial cost ($1.5 to $5 billion).

With regard to apportioning risk and liability among the various entities involved in the project (i.e., the public; the property owners; the national, state,
and local governmental and regulatory agencies; the transit authority; and the
planners, designers, construction managers, contractors, suppliers, and others),
project elements must be identified and their influence upon the apportionment
duly assessed.

The owning authority is governed by a 10-man board of directors representing
four major regional areas. Within each regional area there are several incorporated communities and special single-purpose districts (e.g., a sanitary

district). These political entities are governed by elected or appointed bodies whose views may change as membership changes. The system's alignment will traverse the jurisdiction of most of these communities and districts.

Eminent domain powers have been granted to the transit authority since it is anticipated that much property condemnation will be required. However, the transit authority's policy is to negotiate purchases if at all possible.

Construction will require street closures and traffic control. Within the several communities involved there are active and powerful commercial associations and neighborhood groups. The access to many smaller commercial firms will be disrupted during the course of construction.

A "no strike" labor agreement has been signed by the authority and the area's labor unions. Similarly, agreements for collector type service and transfer of patrons are to be worked out and signed with the several community bus systems now in operation. The location and extent of future extensions of the transit system have not yet been agreed to by all affected communities.

The transit authority has taken a strong stand on the matters of affirmative action and equal employment opportunity regarding minorities. In some construction specialties, there are limited numbers of minority-owned firms within reasonable geographical limits (e.g., in two cases, only one firm is available).

Several means are being used to finance the system. General obligation bonds will provide most of the local funds; however, there will be a special sales tax, the proceeds of which will be used to ensure certain funding. Federal and state grants are expected to provide the majority of project funds but not all features of the proposed project have the full concurrence of federal review authorities. Nonfederally approved items included will have to be completely locally funded. By the time construction starts, it is doubtful whether a fare system will have been adopted or policy established regarding such things as possible parking lot charges. The transit authority has elected to be self-insured up to $3 million and plans to implement a "wrap-up" insurance program for the construction elements.

The transit authority plans to prohibit public access and physically secure the entrances to system property and facilities during nonoperating hours. In commercial areas, there will be entrances from the transit property to cooperating stores or buildings to provide for patron convenience and commercial enhancement. Concept level car design for the system envisions using the latest available safety and comfort features. Control of the system's vehicle operations is to be automatic with high-frequency service during the peak hours which, in turn, dictates short headings between trains. Several branchings of the system will require "Y's" with appropriate control and safety features.

Terrain and geology vary throughout the area to be traversed by the system. Construction work will be of at-grade, aerial, subaqueous, and tunnel types with stations being located in all except the subaqueous areas. Tunneling will be through sandy soils, rock, and mixed face areas. It is likely that certain lengths of tunnel will have to be constructed under high air pressure conditions because of water conditions, but other lengths could be built in free air if freezing or chemical grouting are employed. The soils investigation carried out by the transit authority's agents has been reasonably thorough.

The transit authority has been successful in securing master agreements with area utilities regarding relocation, reconstruction, and betterments. Similar agreements relate to the affected railroads and static highways. Local road reconstructions will be decided on a case-by-case basis as plans are submitted for agency review or approval.

POWER PLANT WORKSHOP
FEBRUARY 15-16, 1977

CHAIRMAN

John Tillinghast, Senior Vice President, Engineering and Construction, American Electric Power Company, New York, New York

PARTICIPANTS

Owners

Peter Benzinger, Vice President, Generation, Potomac Electric Power Company, Washington, D.C.
Bruce R. Laverty, Manager, Construction and Transmission Substation Engineering, Southern California Edison Company, Rosemead, California
C. H. Sedam, Vice President, General Construction, Pacific Gas and Electric Company, San Francisco, California

Designers

Edgar E. Erlandson, Senior Construction Manager, Stone & Webster Engineering Corp., Boston, Massachusetts
W. B. Schields, Vice President and General Manager, Gilbert/Commonwealth Associates, Jackson, Michigan
Peter H. Smith, Chairman, Gibbs & Hill, Inc., New York, New York

Contractors

Robert N. Brite, Vice President, Martin K. Eby Construction Company, Omaha, Nebraska
T. A. Nemzek, Vice President and Senior Energy Advisor, J. A. Jones Construction Company, Charlotte, North Carolina

Manufacturers

George R. Brown, Region Manager-Mechanical and Nuclear Services, Installation and Service Engineering Division, General Electric Company, Philadelphia, Pennsylvania
Paul L. McGill, Vice President, Commercial Nuclear Power, Combustion Engineering, Inc., Windsor, Connecticut

Labor

O. L. Kerth, International Representative, Construction and Maintenance Department, International Brotherhood of Electrical Workers, Washington, D.C.

H. Allyn Parmenter, Training Department, United Association of Journeymen & Apprentices of the Plumbing & Pipe Fitting Industry, Washington, D.C.

Insurance

Marshall Ames, Manager, Office for Professional Liability Research, Victor O. Schinnerer & Company, Washington, D.C.

Charles W. Mathers, Vice President, Johnson & Higgins, New York, New York

Legal

John X. Combo, Chief Counsel, Idaho Operations Office, Energy Research and Development Administration, Idaho Falls, Idaho

M. G. Johnson, Counsel for Bechtel Power Corporation, Bechtel Corporation, San Francisco, California

Robert A. Rubin, Partner, Max E. Greenberg, Trayman, Cantor, Reiss & Blasky, New York, New York

Regulatory

Roger S. Boyd, Director, Division of Project Management, Office of Nuclear Reactor Regulation, U.S. Nuclear Regulatory Power Commission, Washington, D.C.

Public Awareness

Philip Mause, Environmental Defense Fund, Washington, D.C.

Mark Messing, Director, Energy Facility Siting, Environmental Policy Institute, Washington, D.C.

LARGE NUCLEAR POWER PROJECT DESCRIPTION

The typical large nuclear power project consists of two physically separated units with an electrical capacity of approximately 1100 MWe each. Each unit utilizes a light water reactor system, a turbine generator, and associated auxiliaries. The facility is located on a 600-acre site adjacent to a navigable river. Each unit is cooled by a separate natural-draft cooling tower with make-up for the cooling tower provided by treated water from the river; blowdown from the cooling tower is discharged to the river.

The principal buildings associated with each unit include the containment structure, the turbine building, and buildings housing the auxiliary systems, the control center, an emergency power supply, the fuel-handling system, and the waste-disposal system.

The containment structure encloses the reactor, the reactor cooling system, and some of the engineered safety systems and supporting systems. The function of the structure is to contain the steam and energy released from an assumed pipe rupture design basis accident and to provide a leak-tight barrier against release of radioactivity from the reactor system during such an accident.

The turbine building houses all auxiliary equipment associated with the main turbine generator. Other auxiliary equipment such as lubricating oil systems and air compressors also are located in this building. No safety-related equipment is housed within the turbine building.

The fuel-handling system consists of a spent-fuel storage pool and fuel receiving and storage area. The handling, loading, and shipping of spent fuel casks and the handling, storage, and transfer to the reactor core of new fuel assemblies are accomplished in this facility.

Floor drain and equipment leakage fluids are collected and processed in a radioactive waste-treatment system before releasing them to the environment. Potentially radioactive gases also are treated and monitored prior to release through the plant vent. Solid wastes are collected and shipped off site in 55-gallon drums.

An on-site reservoir provides make-up for two small mechanical-draft cooling towers that would cool the plant in case the other cooling systems fail.

The reactor system, turbine-generator, and other equipment in the plant are very similar to that utilized in a number of other nuclear plants, which will go into operation prior to these units, with a few modifications to avoid repeating recent unfavorable operating experience.

The typical site is located approximately 10 miles from the edge of an incorporated area with 50,000 inhabitants. Extensive investigations indicate that the site is apparently stable seismically. The site has been investigated in detail to determine the effects of the environment on the plant including extreme temperatures, extreme winds, storms, hurricanes, and floods and the effects of transportation accidents on nearby highways and railroads.

The site must be reviewed in detail and approved by state regulatory agencies; public hearings are involved in the review procedure. The safety of the facility must be reviewed in even greater detail by the U.S. Nuclear Regulatory Commission and a construction permit received before major site construction proceeds. This safety review is probably the most detailed review performed by any federal or state agency for any type of activity. Public hearings with possibly intense opposition are expected for this facility.

The project schedule is approximately 10 years with construction scheduled to start 3 years after initiation of the project. Unit 2 will go into commercial operation approximately one year after Unit 1. The total project cost is in excess of $1.3 billion without future escalation.

WATER RESOURCE DEVELOPMENT WORKSHOP

MARCH 15-16, 1977

CHAIRMAN

Frederick J. Clarke, Lt. General, U.S. Army (Retired), Former Chief, Corps of Engineers, Washington, D.C.

PARTICIPANTS

Owners

G. Stanley Bates, Superintendent, Station Construction, Pacific Gas and Electric Company, San Francisco, California

Jake Douma, Chief, Hydraulic and Hydrology Branch, Directorate of Civil Works, U.S. Army Corps of Engineers, Washington, D.C.

Donald A. Giampoli, Assistant Commissioner, Resource Development, Bureau of Reclamation, U.S. Department of the Interior, Washington, D.C.

Designers

Wilson Binger, Senior Partner and Chairman, Tippetts-Abbett-McCarthy-Stratton, New York, New York

Edward M. Fucik, Chairman Emeritus, Harza Engineering Company, Chicago, Illinois

Dwight L. Glasscock, Vice President and General Manager, Hydro and Water Resources Division, Charles T. Main, Inc., Boston, Massachusetts

Contractors

George T. McCoy, Senior Vice President, Guy F. Atkinson Company, San Francisco, California

Lee Rowe, Vice President, Peter Kiewit Sons' Company, Omaha, Nebraska

Manufacturers

Richard A. Barton, Vice President and General Council, Chicago Bridge and Iron Company, Oak Brook, Illinois

Goetz E. Pfafflin, General Manager, Hydro Turbin Division, Allis Chalmers Corp., York, Pennsylvania

Labor

Allan Burch, Director of Safety, International Union of Operating Engineers, Washington, D.C.

H. Allyn Parmenter, Training Department, United Association of Journeymen & Apprentices of the Plumbing & Pipe Fitting Industry, Washington, D.C.

Insurance

Norman A. Burgoon, Jr., Executive Vice President, Fidelity and Deposit
  Company of Maryland, Baltimore, Maryland
Edward B. Howell, President, Design Professionals Insurance Company and Risk
  Analysis & Research Corporation, San Francisco, California
Henry J. Trainor, President, San Francisco Division, Corroon & Black-Miller &
  Ames, San Francisco, California

Legal

John R. Little, Jr., Regional Solicitor, Department of Interior, Denver, Colorado
Darrell McCrory, Partner, Monteleone & McCrory, Los Angeles, California
Ralph Nash, Professor of Law, The National Law Center, George Washington
  University, Washington, D.C.

Regulatory

Desloge Brown, Chief, Inspections Branch, Division of Licensed Projects, Division
  of Bureau of Power, Federal Power Commission, Washington, D.C.
William Dickerson, Assistant Director, Office of Federal Activities for Resources
  Division Staff, Environmental Protection Agency, Washington, D.C.

Public Awareness

Brent Blackwelder, Chairman, League of Conservation Voters and Washington Repre-
  sentative, Environmental Policy Center, Washington, D.C.
Celia L. Epting, Staff Specialist in Environmental Quality, League of Women
  Voters, Washington, D.C.

WATER RESOURCE DEVELOPMENT PROJECT DESCRIPTION

The project is a large multipurpose dam and reservoir to be constructed in a
semi-remote area in the upper portion of a large river basin. The proposed
dam would be on a free flowing stream and would form a 30,000-acre lake.
Actual construction will be by private contractor. A federal agency would
assume ownership and responsibility for operation and maintenance after construction is completed. The responsible for agency will design the project
and perform supervision and inspection functions during construction to
ensure that the project is constructed in accordance with the plans and specifications. Consulting firms will be used to design some subfeatures of the
project, to perform geotechnical investigations, and to design relocations.
Relocations of utilities and highways, etc., will be performed by owners on
a reimbursable basis. Individual consultants and consulting boards will be
employed on major features, particularly on foundations and grouting. After
construction, periodic inspection of the major features will be performed to
ensure that the project is safe and that it is functioning as designed. The
following relocations will be required by construction of the project: 150
family residences, 3 state highways, 1 interstate highway; numerous power and
telephone lines, 5 pipelines (2 gas and 3 oil); several small cemeteries (500
graves); and 2 railroads.

Due to the extensive impact of the project on the area, many public meetings are to be held throughout the planning and design phase of project development. These meetings will be held in the proposed reservoir area and in the communities located downstream of the dam site where most of the benefits from project construction are expected to be realized. Impact studies will be conducted by consultants.

The project will require about three years to plan and design and another six to eight years to construct. The cost of the project will be about $500 million.

Major structural features of the project are an earth and rockfill dam 300 feet high and 1,800 feet long at the crest, a power plant, and a gated spillway. A low-level sluice will be constructed to permit emptying of the reservoir should it be required.

A small city (less than 10,000 population) is located a short distance downstream of the dam. Larger cities and many small communities are located along the approximately 300 miles of stream between the dam site and the river's mouth, where a large industrial city is located on the seacoast.

The project is located in an area where cavernous limestone is known to exist and is within a few miles of a well documented, but not presently active, geologic fault line.

The reservoir will inundate an important early iron works. The site is considered to be of historical significance because of its age and the unusually well preserved remains of the furnace. There are known archeological sites of some importance in the reservoir area; however, the full significance of these sites and others that are expected to exist is not known. Funds have been authorized for an extensive archeological investigation of the reservoir concurrently with planning and design of the project. The reservoir area also is home to some 30 endangered species, both plant and animal. The 30 miles of free flowing stream to be inundated by the reservoir also is significant due to its great scenic value and excellent white-water canoeing and fishing areas that are enjoyed by large numbers of sportsmen from highly populated areas located within a day's drive of the project site.

The project has been authorized by the U.S. Congress for construction to meet the following needs of the region:

1. Reduce damages due to flooding of the urban areas located along the river as well as the rich agricultural lands located in the mid- to lower-reaches of the river.

2. Generate hydroelectric power--both conventional and pumped storage hydroelectric power will be produced. The pumped storage (peaking power) provision will require the construction of a re-regulating dam downstream of the main dam to regulate flows in the river and to provide a lower pool for pumping in off-peak hours.

3. Provide municipal and industrial water supply--the water is to be drawn both directly from the reservoir and from the river below the dam by communities and industries located along the stream.

4. Provide water-oriented recreation--planned development includes facilities for picnicing, camping, swimming, boating, water skiing, and fishing. In addition, several areas will be leased to concessionaires for marina- and vacation-type development.

5. Provide irrigation water--storage will be provided for irrigation water that will be drawn directly from the reservoir as well as from the river below the dam.

6. Mitigate fish and wildlife damage--in order to mitigate damages to fish and wildlife habitat, a fishery will be built and lands will be purchased and managed by a state agency.

The state in which the project is located has agreed to provide assurance of local cooperation insofar as the overall project is concerned and to participate in the development of the recreational facilities in accordance with the authorizing document for the project and applicable federal laws regarding cost sharing.

A water district is being formed that will have authority to sign a water supply contract with the government and will sell the water to the various users (municipalities, farmers cooperatives, and industries). Through these proceeds, the water district will repay the government over a 50-year period.

The hydroelectric power generated by the project will be marketed by an agency of the federal government. Some of the power will be sold to a local cooperative and some to private power companies. The costs of including hydroelectric power in a multipurpose project also will be reimbursed over a 50-year period.

APPENDIX B

BIOGRAPHICAL INFORMATION
ON
WORKSHOP AND CONFERENCE PARTICIPANTS

BRAB STEERING COMMITTEE

ON RESPONSIBILITY, LIABILITY AND ACCOUNTABILITY FOR RISKS IN CONSTRUCTION

Chairman

JOHN A. WURZ, AIA, Vice President, Cadre Corporation, Atlanta, Georgia. Mr. Wurz, a registered architect in 17 states, formerly served with Heery and Heery, Inc., which he joined in 1963 as project manager and assumed the position of senior vice president, general manager, industrial division. His diversified experience includes design and construction of air fields, airports, industrial facilities, and navigational aids; construction management applications; and the legal ramifications of architect's and engineer's activities. He received degrees in science and architecture from the Georgia Institute of Technology and in environmental planning from Stanford University.

Members

JOHN P. BUEHLER, Consultant, Bechtel Incorporated, San Francisco, California. Mr. Buehler has been associated with Bechtel since 1955 and served as vice president and manager of the firm's Hydro and Community Facilities Division from 1962 to 1975 with overall responsibility for business development, engineering studies, and design and project management for water-resource-related development, transportation, and community facilities projects. He served in the U.S. Army Corps of Engineers from 1934 to 1955 and retired as a colonel. He received degrees in civil engineering from the U.S. Military Academy and Massachusetts Institute of Technology and attended the U.S. Army Command and General Staff College and Joint Army-Navy Staff College.

WALTER S. DOUGLAS, FASCE, retired Chairman, Parsons, Brinckerhoff, Quade and Douglas, New York, New York. Mr. Douglas worked with PBQ&D since 1939 and was involved in airport construction engineering design; underground construction of rapid transit systems, tunnels, waterways and harbors; and foundation engineering. He is a member of the National Academy of Engineering and the Executive Committee of the Building Research Advisory Board and is past chairman of the BRAB Federal Construction Council and past vice president of the American Institute of Consulting Engineers. He received a liberal arts degree from Dartmouth College and a civil engineering degree from Harvard University.

ROBERT A. GEORGINE, President, Building and Construction Trades Department, AFL-CIO, Washington, D.C. Mr. Georgine began his career with Lathers' Local 74 in 1953 and became the international representative of the Wood, Wire, and Metal Lathers' International Union in 1963 and the general president in 1970. He was elected secretary-treasurer of the Building and Construction Trades Department in 1971 and assumed his present position in 1974. He is a member of the Building Research Advisory Board, the National Institute of Building Sciences, and the National Bureau of Standards Building Technology Advisory Committee and has served on the Construction Industry Stabilization Committee and the Advisory Council on Employee Welfare and Pension Benefit Plans of the Department of Labor. He also is chairman of the National Coordinating Committee for Multiemployer Plants.

BEN C. GERWICK, Jr., FASCE, Professor, Construction Engineering, University of California, San Francisco, California, and engineering consultant for major bridge and marine construction projects and ocean structures. Mr. Gerwick is a member of the National Academy of Engineering Marine Board, Federation Internationale de la Precontrainte, and Association Francaise du Beton and is past president of the Prestressed Concrete Institute. He received a civil engineering degree from the University of California.

JOHN P. GNAEDINGER, President and Co-founder, Soil Testing Services, Inc., Northbrook, Illinois, which specializes in soils investigation, engineering reports, laboratory testing, and structural foundation design involving highway, airfield, dam, sewer, water supply, dock facility, and building projects. He has been active in the development and evaluation of the professional liability aspects of design professionals and of insurance for professionals. He is past chairman of the Building Research Advisory Board and serves on numerous technical committees of professional societies. He received civil engineering degrees from Cornell University and Northwestern University.

SAMUEL L. HACK, Director, Office of Construction and Facility Management, U.S. Department of Energy, Washington, D.C. Mr. Hack is responsible for the construction and facilities management program of the Department, as he had been under the Energy Research and Development Administration. The Department's major facilities include production plants for nuclear materials and weapons and research, development and demonstration plants and laboratories. He served the former Atomic Energy Commission since 1953 in numerous legal, contractual, and managerial assignments. He was president of the Montgomery County, Maryland, Chapter of the Federal Bar Association. He received a degree in chemical engineering from the University of Michigan and a LL.B from Harvard Law School; he also was awarded a Mid-Career Fellowship by Princeton University's Woodrow Wilson School of Public and International Affairs.

R. M. MONTI, FASCE, Chief Engineer, The Port Authority of New York and New Jersey, New York, New York. Mr. Monti, a registered professional engineer in New York and New Jersey, joined the Port Authority in 1952 and has engaged in engineering and construction management of port, airport, marine terminal, and transportation facilities under the jurisdiction of the Port Authority.

He formerly was construction manager of the World Trade Center, 1964-1972; commander of the Civil Engineer Corps, U.S. Navy; director of the Society of American Military Engineers; and Secretary of the New York Construction Users Council. He received a civil engineering degree from Manhattan College.

LOUIS W. RIGGS, FASCE, President, Tudor Engineering Company, San Francisco, California. Mr. Riggs joined Tudor in 1951 and has been involved in the planning and engineering design of highways, bridges, dams, port works, military facilities, and rapid transit and other transportation systems. He is a member of the Board of Control of Parsons-Brinckerhoff-Tudor-Bechtel, a joint venture responsible for the BART Systems (San Francisco), MARTA (Atlanta), and urban transportation systems in Caracas, Singapore, and other cities. He received a civil engineering degree from the University of California.

WORKSHOP CHAIRMEN

FREDERICK J. CLARKE, FASCE, Lt. General, U.S. Army (Retired), and consultant to Tippetts-Abbett-McCarthy-Stratton, Washington, D.C. General Clark served in the Army since 1937 as district engineer in Pakistan (1957-1959); on the Engineering Command Staff, Washington, D.C. (1960-1963); as director of military construction (1963-1965); as commanding general, Army Engineering Center, Fort Belvoir (1965-1966); and as chief, U.S. Army Corps of Engineers (1969-1973). He is a member of the National Academy of Engineering and the International Committee on Large Dams and is past chairman of the Washington Metropolitan Area Transit Commission. He received degrees from the U.S. Military Academy and Cornell University in civil engineering and from Harvard Advanced Management School.

B. R. STOKES, Executive Director, American Public Transit Association, Washington, D.C., the national organization representing the urban transit industry in the United States, Canada, and Mexico. Mr. Stokes is responsible for directing all planning and policy analysis, technical and research, governmental, administrative and member, and communication services. He formerly served as chief executive officer (1963-1974) of the San Francisco Bay Area Transit and as consultant to the U.S. Secretary of Transportation, U.S. Department of Housing and Urban Development, and California Governor's Task Force on Transportation. He is a member of the National Research Council Transportation Research Board. He received his degree from the University of California.

JOHN TILLINGHAST, FASCE, Vice President, Engineering and Construction, American Electric Power Corporation, New York, New York, which acts for subsidiaries in engineering and managerial functions. Mr. Tillinghast, a registered professional engineer in serveral states, joined the corporation in 1949 and is responsible for all engineering and construction activities for all components of the company's system, which operates in a seven-state (Indiana, Kentucky, Michigan, Ohio, Tennessee, Virginia and West Virginia) area. He is a member of the National Academy of Engineering and the Institute of Electrical and Electronic Engineers. He received degrees in mechanical engineering from Columbia University.

WORKSHOP PARTICIPANTS

Owners and Managers

WILLIAM D. ALEXANDER, FASCE, Assistant General Manager, Transit Division, Atlanta Rapid Transit Authority, Atlanta, Georgia. Since 1975, Mr. Alexander has been responsible for the design, engineering, and construction of Atlanta's rapid transit system. A registered professional engineer in 11 states, he possesses broad experience in engineering and construction as an owner, designer, project manager, and director. He has directed the design and construction of the Fermi National Accelerator Laboratory, managed the design of the Vehicle Assembly Building at Cape Kennedy, and served as chief of facilities design for the Atlas, Titan, and Minuteman ballistic missle programs. He retired as a colonel from the U.S. Air Force and received a civil engineering degree from North Carolina State University and a bachelor of science degree in chemistry from the Virginia Military Institute.

G. STANLEY BATES, Superintendent, Station Construction, Pacific Gas and Electric Company, San Francisco, California. Mr. Bates, a registered professional engineer in California, has 25 years of experience in managing the construction of dams; tunnels; penstocks; and hydroelectric, fossil, and nuclear power plants. He is a member of the Legislative Committee of the Associated General Contractors, of the Pacific Coast Electric Association, and of the Pacific Coast Gas Association. He was nominated as an Alfred P. Sloan Fellow at Stanford Graduate School of Business and received a civil engineering degree from Heald Engineering College.

PETER BENZINGER, Vice President, Generation, Potomac Electric Power Company, Washington, D.C. Having joined the company in 1949 and having served in various capacities in the engineering and operating departments including plant superintendent of the Chalk Point and Dickerson Generating Stations, Mr. Benzinger now is responsible for engineering and operation of steam electric stations and recently has given a great deal of attention to environmental matters. A registered professional engineer in Maryland and the District of Columbia, he is a member of the American Society of Mechanical Engineers and received an engineering degree from Princeton University.

ROY T. DODGE, Chief of Design and Construction, Washington Metropolitan Area Transit Authority, Washington, D.C. Since 1967, Mr. Dodge has been responsible for the Authority's engineering, architectural, and program control and construction and equipment design offices and serves as contracting officer for all design and construction activities. He retired as a brigadier general after a 29-year career with the U.S. Army Corps of Engineers that included supervision of military and civil construction across 13 northern states. He is former chairman of the U.S. section of four international boards controlling the international waters of the Great Lakes. He received a mechanical engineering degree from Auburn University and an industrial engineering degree from Cornell University and also attended the U.S. Army War College and the Advanced Management Program at Harvard University.

JACOB H. DOUMA, Chief, Hydraulic and Hydrology Branch, U.S. Army Corps of Engineers, Office of the Chief of Engineers, Washington, D.C. Mr. Douma, a registered professional engineer in Virginia, is responsible for final review and approval of all the Corps' hydraulic design and research programs and serves as top technical advisor to the Corps' division, district, and hydraulic laboratories on hydraulic planning, design, research, and operation for multipurpose dams, flood control channels, inland waterways, navigation locks, and dams and coastal engineering projects. He is a member of the National Academy of Engineering.

DONALD A. GIAMPOLI, Assistant Commissioner, Resource Development, Bureau of Reclamation, U.S. Department of the Interior, Washington, D.C. Mr. Giampoli, a registered professional engineer, joined the Bureau in 1975 and oversees the Bureau's multi-million dollar construction program and the Division of Research. He formerly served as an official of Associated General Contractors Association (1960-1974) and as an urban highway design engineer for the District of Columbia Highway Department (1957-1959). He received degrees in civil engineering from Santa Clara University and Catholic University.

JOHN F. HOBAN, Deputy Director, Rail Transportation Department, The Port Authority of New York and New Jersey, New York, New York. Mr. Hoban, a registered professional engineer in New York and New Jersey, has served the Port Authority since 1954 and has been associated with the Port Authority Trans-Hudson Corporation (PATH) since 1962. Before assuming his present position, he was superintendent of rail programs and general superintendent of rail operations. He currently is project director of PATH New Jersey Rail Projects. He received civil engineering degrees from Manhattan College and Columbia University.

BRUCE R. LAVERTY, FASCE, Manager, Construction and Transmission, Substation Engineering, Engineering and Construction Department, California Edison Company, Rosemead, California. Mr. Laverty, a registered civil engineer in California, is responsible for design and construction of the company's transmission lines and substations and construction management services for thermal generating projects and a nuclear project. He has served in various engineering and construction management assignments for hydroelectric, steam electric, and nuclear projects including the Vermillion Dam and the Mammoth Poll and San Onofre projects. He received civil engineering degrees from the University of Washington and Cornell University.

JOHN T. O'NEILL, Executive Officer for Construction Administration and Chief Engineer, New York City Transit Authority, New York, New York, and Colonel, U.S. Army (Retired). Mr. O'Neill, a registered professional engineer in three states, joined the Transit Authority in 1970; formerly he served as New York Commissioner of Buildings (1967-1970), director of engineering, for the New York World's Fair (1964-1967), and consulting engineer to the Triborough Bridge and Tunnel Authority (1961-1964). He received a civil engineering degree from the University of Maryland and attended the U.S. Army Command and General Staff College.

CHARLES H. SEDAM, Vice President, General Construction, Pacific Gas and Electric Company, San Francisco, California. Mr. Sedam joined the company in 1964 and is past director of the Pacific Coast Electrical Association, past director of the IEEE, and past state director of the Associated General Contractors. He is a member of the Pacific Coast Gas Association, Construction Committee Business Roundtable, and EEI Construction Task Force. He received an electrical engineering degree from the University of Washington and attended the Executive Development Program of the Stanford University Graduate School of Business.

Designers

WILSON V. BINGER, FASCE, Partner and Chairman, Tippetts-Abbett-McCarthy-Stratton (TAMS) Consulting Engineers and Architects, New York, New York. Having joined the firm in 1952, Mr. Binger's major responsibility was the Tarbela Dam project in Pakistan. His career has included work with the U.S. Army Corps of Engineers, the Panama Canal, two years as a contractor in bridge construction, and several engineering assignments in South America. He has served for 15 years as secretary of the U.S. Committee on Large Dams (USCOLD) and six years as a member of its executive committee. He is a member of two committees of the International Commission on Large Dams and the National Academy of Engineering and is a fellow of the Institution of Civil Engineers, director of the International Road Federation, and treasurer and member of the U.S. National Committee for the International Federation for Documentation, Executive Committee. He received arts and science degrees from Harvard University.

JAMES A. CAYWOOD, Senior Vice President and Director, DeLeuw, Cather and Company, Washington, D.C. Mr. Caywood, a registered professional engineer in 25 states and the District of Columbia, presently is project director for the prime architect/engineer contractor responsible for all architectural and engineering services needed to implement the $1.75 billion Rail Passenger Improvement Program on the Northeast Corridor between Washington, D.C., and Boston. He formerly served as project manager for the 98-mile Washington Metro System and as chief engineer and general manager of engineer planning for the C&O/B&O Railroad. He is a member of numerous professional societies and received an engineering degree from the University of Kentucky.

PAUL E. CONRAD, Executive Vice President, Wilbur Smith and Associates, Columbia, South Carolina. Mr. Conrad, a registered professional engineer in 13 states, is responsible for administration and coordination of the operating regions of the firm. Having joined the firm in 1955, he has participated in the executive, coordination, and management of a variety of highway and rail transportation, urban and regional planning, and land development projects throughout the United States. He is a member of numerous professional societies and received a civil engineering degree from the University of Connecticut.

EDGAR E. ERLANDSON, Senior Construction Manager, Stone and Webster Engineering Corporation, Boston, Massachusetts. Mr. Erlandson, a registered professional engineer in Massachusetts, joined the corporation in 1941 as a mechanical designer and in his current position has been involved in the construction of nuclear and fossil fuel power projects throughout the eastern United States. He received mechanical engineering and management development degrees from Northeastern University.

JOHN E. EVERSON, Chairman, Parsons, Brinckerhoff, Quade & Douglas, Inc., San Francisco, California. Since 1959 Mr. Everson, a registered professional engineer in eight states and Canada, has been responsible primarily for West Coast and Pacific Basin projects. He served as project director of the BART transit project for the Parsons-Brinckerhoff-Tudor-Bechtel joint venture and is chairman of the Board of Control for Parsons, Brinckerhoff, Quade & Douglas, Inc.,Tudor Engineering Company, a joint venture for the MARTA transit project in Atlanta, Georgia. He received a civil engineering degree from Rensselaer Polytechnic Institute.

E. MONTFORD FUCIK, FASCE, FAAAS, Chairman Emeritus, Harza Engineering, Chicago, Illinois, a consulting engineering firm of 1000 engineers, scientists, and support personnel specializing in the planning and design of water resource, land, and power development projects (e.g., dams, regional and river basins, flood control and drainage, water supply and wastewater treatment, land irrigation and drainage, reclamation, soil conservation, tunnels and underground structures, transportation, and power generation and transmission). He joined the firm in 1945 and recently retired as chief executive officer. He is a member of the International Commission on Irrigation and Drainage, the U.S. Committee on Irrigation, Drainage and Flood Control, the U.S. Committee on Large Dams, the U.S. National Committee for the World Energy Conference, the Independent Panel to Review the Cause of the Teton Dam Failure, the National Academy of Engineering, and numerous professional societies. He received a civil engineering degree from Princeton University and an engineering degree from Harvard University. He is a registered professional engineer in 11 states and Canada.

DWIGHT L. GLASSCOCK, Vice President and General Manager, Hydro and Water Resource Division, Charles T. Main, Inc., Boston, Massachusetts. Mr. Glasscock joined the firm in 1952 and is responsible for direction of his division's activities in the United States, South America, Africa, and Asia. His experience includes project management and design direction for a major water resource development in Brazil; atomic power development at Brookhaven National Laboratory and Cambridge; economic studies and analyses for the St. Lawrence Power Project, the California Water Plan, and the Niagra Power Project; and power resources and requirements studies for the Province of Nova Scotia. He received a civil engineering degree from the University of Illinois.

DAVID G. HAMMOND, FASCE, Vice President, Daniel, Mann, Johnson and Mendenhall, Baltimore, Maryland. Mr. Hammond currently is program director for rapid transit in the Eastern Region. As assistant general manager for Engineering Operations, he had overall charge for design and construction of the BART system. He formerly served 25 years with U.S. Army Corps of Engineers in such positions of chief of research and development, chief of engineer division for the Continental Command, and chief of installations for the Army Command in Europe. He is a member of the National Research Council U.S. National Committee on Tunneling Technology and has served on numerous study, research, and development committees. He received degrees from Pennsylvania State University and Cornell University in civil engineering and from the U.S. Army Command and General Staff College.

ROBERT S. O'NEIL, Senior Vice President and Project Manager, DeLeuw, Cather and Company, Washington, D.C. Mr. O'Neil, a registered professional engineer in nine states, he is responsible for the firm's Mid-Atlantic Region including general engineering for the Washington Metropolitan Area Rail Rapid Transit System and Train Control and Communication Systems for Baltimore Transit System. He joined the firm in 1960 and has been involved in engineering, organization, and project management of highway, port, rail, and transit systems. He is a member of the American Society of Civil Engineers, American Public Transit Association, American Railway Engineering Association, and National Research Council Transportation Research Board Committee on Rail Systems Planning and Development. He received mechanical engineering degrees from Notre Dame University, Catholic University, and the University of Chicago.

W. B. SCHIELDS, Vice President and General Manager for Power Engineering, Gilbert/Commonwealth Associates, Jackson, Michigan. Mr. Schields, a registered professional engineer in four states, is responsible for design and engineering of all nuclear, fossil fuel, and gas projects and for supervising the managers of the mechanical, electrical, structural, specialties, and drafting departments and five senior project managers. Possessing over eight years of professional experience in power engineering, he recently has been involved in all aspects of nuclear and power generating station design, station licensing efforts, nuclear standards and computer applications development, project and department management supervision, and area marketing. He received electrical engineering degrees from Lehigh University, Bowdoin College, and the Massachusetts Institute of Technology.

PETER H. SMITH, Chairman, Gibbs and Hill, Inc., New York, New York, an engineering and constructor firm involved in nuclear, fossil, and hydroelectric power generation; transportation electrification; environmental engineering; architecture and urban development; and industrial and civil works. He also serves as president of Dravo Utility Constructors, Inc.; chairman and director of Gibbs and Hill subsidiary companies; and consultant to Electricite de France, Enel-Italy, and the IAEA-Third Party Liability Committee. He received degrees in engineering and architecture and planning from Renesslaer Polytechnic Institute.

ELLIS E. WILHOYT, JR., Project Manager, Bechtel Associates Professional Corporation, Washington, D.C., which has served as general construction consultants to the Washington Metropolitan Area Transit Authority since 1971. Mr. Wilhoyt joined Bechtel in 1967 as assistant project director for Parsons-Brinckerhoff-Tudor-Bechtel, the joint venture of engineers on the BART project. He formerly served 30 years with the U.S. Army Corps of Engineers. He is a registered professional engineer in California, Washington, D.C., and Virginia and received a civil engineering degree from the University of California.

Contractors

CHARLES H. ATHERTON, Vice President and Area Manager, J. F. Shea Company, Bethesda, Maryland. Having joined the firm in 1966 as manager of the San Francisco Bay Area Rapid Transit System station and tunnel project, Mr. Atherton currently is responsible for Washington Metropolitan Area Transit Authority construction projects totaling $125 million and for bidding on the East Coast. He formerly served the Perini Corporation as general superintendent of highway construction and carried out various air base, power dam, seaway, and tunneling project assignments. He received mechanical engineering degrees from the University of Virginia and Tulane University.

ROBERT N. BRITE, Vice President and Area Manager, Martin K. Eby Construction Company, Inc., Omaha, Nebraska. Mr. Brite possesses 26 years of experience in all phases of construction and has served as field engineer, superintendent, estimator, project manager, and area manager with extensive work in power plant construction. He received civil engineering and architectural engineering degrees from the University of Oklahoma.

GEORGE A. FOX, FASCE, Executive Vice President and Chief Engineer, Grow-Tunneling Corporation, New York, New York, a subsidiary of Alpha Portland Industries which is engaged in subway and tunnel work and specializes in heavy construction shafts and tunnels. As chairman of the Tunnel Committee and treasurer of the Associated General Contractors of New York City, Mr. Fox has been deeply involved in employer-employee relations, especially with Tunnel Workers Union (Local 147). He is a member of the Employer Trustee Welfare Fund and chairman of the Trustees Retirement Fund Local 147, chairman of the Contact Administration Committee of the American Society of Civil Engineers, Construction Division, and a member of the Contracting Practices Subcommittee of the National Research Council. He received civil engineering degrees from Cooper Union and Brooklyn Polytechnic Institute. He is a registered professional engineer in New York and New Jersey.

RICHARD E. HALL, President, Underground Construction Company, Inc., San Leandro, California. Mr. Hall, a registered professional engineer in two states and a licensed general contractor in eight states and the District of Columbia, is past president of the Associated General Contractors (AGC) of California, chairman of the Western Federation of Regional Construction Employers, vice chairman of the Western Chapters Conference of the AGC, and a member of the AGC Collective Bargaining, Long Range Planning, Municipal-Utilities Committee. He received a civil engineering degree from the University of California.

GEORGE T. MCCOY, Senior Vice President, Guy F. Atkinson Company, San Francisco, California. Mr. McCoy, a registered professional engineer in California, is responsible for the company's General Construction Group including Atkinson-International (Aust.) Limited, Walsh Construction Company, Commonwealth Construction Company, and Atkinson Dynamics Company and has been involved in private contracting with the firm since 1952. He formerly served as district construction engineer in charge of all construction for the Central Coastal District, California Division of Highways. He received a civil engineer degree from Stanford University.

138

THOMAS A. NEMZEK, Vice President and Senior Energy Advisor , J. A. Jones Construction Company, Charlotte, North Carolina. Mr. Nemzek formerly served as director of the Division of Reactor Research and Development, and as consultant to the U.S. Energy Research and Development Administration, who was responsible for directing national civilian reactor activities and technological support and worked for the Atomic Energy Commission at its Richland, San Francisco, and Chicago Operations Offices. He received a nuclear engineering degree from North Carolina State University and attended the Federal Executive Institute.

LEE ROWE, Vice President, Peter Kiewit Sons' Company, Omaha, Nebraska. Having joined the firm in 1949, Mr. Rowe is responsible for management of operating districts involved in dam, power, water treatment, petrochemical plant, and underground construction in the United States and Canada. He formerly served the firm as engineer, foreman, superintendent, and project manager and was involved in dam construction, aggregate production, channel excavation, reservoir construction, and estimating for water resource projects in United States and Canada. He received a civil engineering degree from the University of Illinois.

GEORGE J. TAMARO, Vice President and Chief Engineer, ICOS Corporation of America, New York, New York. Mr. Tamaro, a registered professional engineer in four states and the District of Columbia, is involved in the promotion, estimating, bidding, design, and technical implementation aspects of the firm's slurry wall construction tunneling work. He formerly spent two years doing engineering research at Lehigh University and eleven years with the Port Authority of New York and New Jersey where he was involved in planning, design, and supervision of construction for the World Trade Center. He is a member of numerous professional societies and received civil engineering degrees from Manhattan College and Lehigh University and an architectural technology degree from Columbia University.

Manufacturers and Suppliers

RICHARD A. BARTON, Vice President and General Counsel, Chicago Bridge and Iron Company, Oak Brook Illinois. Having joined the firm in 1949, Mr. Barton has served as assistant counsel, counsel for the international Division, and general counsel. He formerly was assistant instructor in engineering at and received civil engineering and law degrees from the University of Missouri.

GEORGE R. BROWN, Regional Manager, Mechanical and Nuclear Service, Installation and Service Engineering Division, General Electric Company, Philadelphia, Pennsylvania, and is responsible for power systems and service operation. Having joined GE in 1957, Mr. Brown served as field engineer, start-up engineer for large steam turbines and generators, field engineering supervisor, specialist for turbine installation practices, manager for methods engineering-mechanical and nuclear, and manager for mechanical and nuclear service. He received a degree in marine engineering from the New York State Maritime College.

EDWARD F. DELANEY, Manager, Turbine Service Programs, Mechanical and Nuclear Service Department, Installations and Service Engineering Division, General Electric Company, Schenectady, New York. Mr. Delaney joined GE in 1940 and is responsible for implementing and coordinating field engineering service programs for GE's gas, steam, medium steam, and mechanical drive turbine activities in utility and industrial markets. Before assuming his present position, he worked in the firm's Northeast Industrial and Marine Division. He received a mechanical engineering degree from Pennsylvania State University.

H. JACK HUNKELE, President, Foley Machinery, Piscataway, New Jersey, which for the past 10 years has supplied heavy construction machinery to contractors for virtually all kinds of construction but especially transportation construction in the Northern New Jersey and New York City areas. He formerly spent 12 years in management at the Caterpillar Tractor Company and was involved in both domestic and international markets. He is a member of the Associated General Contractors and received a degree in industrial engineering from Lehigh University.

A. G. MAIER, Manager, Mass Transit Sales, General Railway Signal Company, New York, New York. Having joined the company in 1945, Mr. Maier is involved in circuit design and engineering, sales engineering, and eastern and western division management. He is a member of the Board of Directors of the American Public Transit Association and past chairman of its Associate Member Division and is a member of the Railway Progress Institute. He received an electrical engineering degree from the Rochester Institute of Technology and a telecommunication degree from Rochester Technical Center.

PAUL L. MCGILL, Vice President, Commercial Nuclear Power, Combustion Engineering, Inc., Windsor, Connecticut. Mr. McGill is responsible for project management, licensing, start-up and follow-on services, planning, and business development. Prior to 1968, he held various engineering and management positions at Bettis Atomic Power Laboratory and Martin Marietta Corporation. He received chemical engineering degrees from the Massachusetts Institute of Technology and Syracuse University.

GOETZ E. PFAFFLIN, General Manager, Hydro-Turbine Division, Allis-Chalmers Corporation, York, Pennsylvania. Having joined the firm in 1961, Mr. Pfafflin is involved in engineering, marketing, and management and travels extensively in Europe, Asia, Africa, South America, and Australia. He received a mechanical engineering degree from McGill University.

Labor

ALAN F. BURCH, Director, Department of Safety and Accident Prevention, International Union of Operating Engineers (IUOE), Washington, D.C. A member of the IUOE since 1946, Mr. Burch served for two years as a member of the Occupational Safety and Health Review Commission. He also has served on numerous American National Standards Institute and National Fire Protection Association committees, has worked with the Society of Automotive Engineers and the American Society of Mechanical Engineers on technical standards,

and has been a member of numerous federal advisory committees dealing
with health and safety. He is a member of the Board of the National
Safety Council and the American National Standards Institute.

O. L. KERTH, International Representative, Construction and Maintenance
Department, International Brotherhood of Electrical Workers (IBEW),
Washington, D.C. Mr. Kerth is responsible for liaison with the Department
of Labor and other federal agencies in connection with the Davis-Bacon and
Service Contract Acts. He began his career as a construction electrician
in IBEW Local 816 (Kentucky) where he eventually served as president. He
is past president of the Paducah Building and Construction Trade Council,
past president of the West Kentucky AFC-CIO Area Council, former Commissioner
of Labor for the State of Kentucky, and member of the International Association of Labor Officials and the Council of Industrial Relations for Electrical Contracting Industry.

JIM E. LAPPING, Director, Safety and Occupational Health, Building and
Construction Trades Department, AFL-CIO, Washington, D.C. Mr. Lapping is
a member of the AFL-CIO Staff Subcommittee on Occupational Safety and
Health, the Building and Construction Trades Department Safety Committee,
the Industrial Union Department Lead Committee, the American Society of
Safety Engineers, the National Safety Management Society, the Society for
Occupational and Environmental Health, and the Construction Safety Association of America. He formerly worked with the Evaluative Research and Organizational Development Program at the University of Oregon and at the International Harvester Process Research Group-Materials Engineering Laboratory
where he worked with design and evaluation test methodology and equipment
for newly developed super alloys. He received degrees in public administration, economics, and evaluative research and research methodology from the
University of Oregon and the U.S. Naval School of Metallurgy.

JOHN M. PARKER, Director, Construction and Maintenance Department, International Brotherhood of Electrical Workers (IBEW), Washington, D.C. Before
assuming his present position in 1960, Mr. Parker served as vice president
of IBEW Local 968, secretary of the Central Labor Council, vice president
of the State Federation (West Virginia), president of the State Building
Trades Council, and secretary of the State Electrical Workers Association.
He also was the international representative of IBEW Fourth District handling
construction matters for such jobs as the Atomic Energy Commission, Waverly,
Ohio, aluminum, power, steel, and chemical plants. He is a member of the
Correlating Committee, National Electrical Code, and the Building Trades
Screening Committee and has served as co-chairman of the Government Procure-
ment Committee and member of the National Joint Board representing specialty
trades.

H. ALLYN PARMENTER, Training Department, United Association of Journeymen
and Apprentices of the Plumbing and Pipe Fitting Industry, Washington, D.C.
Mr. Parmenter is responsible for guiding 600 local training programs in-
volving 34,000 apprentices and journeyman in the United States and Canada.
He was formerly officer and training director of the Joint Apprentice and
Journeyman Training Program in Miami, Florida, and has worked in all phases

of the pipefitting trade as well as with legislators in drafting bills on education and labor and with state and national governmental agencies in solving local problems that require knowledge of administration and laws concerning training, new materials, and processes used in the construction industry.

JOE M. SHORT, Director, Education and Training, Laborers' International Union of North America (LINUA), Washington, D.C. A member of Local 204, Terre Haute, Indiana, since 1949, Mr. Short served as the local's secretary-treasurer for nine years, as secretary-treasurer for the Indiana Building Trades Council for eight years, and as assistant to the secretary-treasurer of the Indiana State District Council for seven years. He also served as national safety director of LINUA's MDTA program and assistant to the general president of LINUA. He is a member of the Construction Safety Advisory Board and the Executive Committee of the National Safety Council as well as vice chairman of the Council's Labor Conference. He received a bachelor of science degree from Indiana State University.

Insurance and Bonding

MARSHALL AMES, Manager, Office for Professional Liability Research, Victor O. Schinnerer and Company, Inc., Washington, D.C., insurance brokers for the Architects' and Engineers Professional Insurance Program and counselors to leading professional designer organizations. Having joined the firm in 1969 as an underwriter, Mr. Ames presently is responsible for expanding loss prevention activities including publication of guidelines for improving practices and a newsletter for design professional counselors. He received a degree in history from Norwich University.

NORMAN A. BURGOON, Jr., Executive Vice President, Fidelity and Deposit Company of Maryland, Baltimore, Maryland, which specializes in bonding. Mr. Burgoon joined the firm in 1935 and also served as vice chairman of the Executive Committee and past chairman of the Contract Bond Advisory Committee of the Surety Association of America. He is a former member of the Executive Committee of the American Insurance Association and past vice president and director of the Bureau of Contract Information, Inc. He received a juris doctorate degree from the University of Baltimore.

WILLIAM C. CULLEN, Vice President, Johnson and Higgins, Washington, D.C., international insurance brokers and employee benefits consultants serving major utilities, nuclear facilities, and transit and steel companies and forerunners in the design of wrap-up insurance having arranged more than 100 wrap-up programs for major projects. Mr. Cullen joined the firm in 1963 with 14 years of prior experience with another New York insurance broker. Director of Metropolitan Insurance Administrators, insurance and safety consultants to Washington Metropolitan Area Transit Authority. He received a degree in economics from the Wharton School of Finance of the University of Pennsylvania and in insurance and corporate finance from New York University.

EDWARD B. HOWELL, President, Design Professionals Insurance Company and Risk Analysis and Research Corporation, San Francisco, California. Mr. Howell specializes in professional liability insurance and loss prevention for consulting engineers in private practice and was the promulgator and instigator of several professional liability loss prevention programs for consulting engineers, architects, soils and foundation engineers, and testing laboratories. He began his insurance career with Employers Insurance Company of Wausau specializing in contractors' and construction risk. A member of the Bar of the State of Wisconsin, he received bachelor of science and juris doctorate degrees from the University of Wisconsin.

HIRAM L. KENNICOTT, Jr., Vice President, Kemper Insurance Companies, and Manager, Commercial Lines Underwriting, Chicago, Illinois. Mr. Kennicott has worked with the organization for 35 years and is a member of the Workers Compensation Committees of the Chamber of Commerce of the United States and the American Mutual Insurance Alliance. He also has served on numerous insurance and insurance-related committees and received a bachelor of science degree from the University of Chicago.

C. W. MATHERS, Vice President, Johnson and Higgins, New York, New York. Mr. Mathers joined the firm in 1969 and is responsible for coordination of nuclear insurance activities. He is a chartered Property Casualty Underwriter (CPCU) and a member of the Atomic Industrial Forum's Insurance Committee and American Nuclear Society. He received a bachelor of arts degree from Bloomfield College and attended advanced power plant technology, nuclear fuels management and economics, and nuclear power management courses courses at the Georgia Institute of Technology.

V. WALLACE RYLAND, President, Fred S. James and Company, Inc. of Virginia, Baltimore, Maryland. Having joined the firm in 1960, Mr. Ryland was instrumental in the formation of the James Transit Unit, which is composed of a group of insurance specialists engaged in research and development in the field of transit insurance management. He has been a member of the American Public Transit Association since its inception and is an active member of the Virginia State Insurance Board. He received a bachelor of arts degree from the American University.

HENRY J. TRAINOR, President, San Francisco Division, Corroon and Black-Miller and Ames, San Francisco, California. Mr. Trainor has spent 40 years in the insurance business, 25 of which are with his present firm, which specializes in bonds and insurance relating to the construction industry. He attended the Wharton School of Finance of the University of Pennsylvania.

Legal

JOHN X. COMBO, Chief Counsel, Idaho Operations Office, U.S. Energy Research and Development Administration, Idaho Falls, Idaho. Mr. Combo has held his current position since 1962 and possesses extensive experience in legal and contractural matters relating to nuclear power production and experimental and testing facilities construction and operation. He formerly served as attorney and chief counsel for the Atomic Energy Commission and attorney and

143

geologist for the U.S. Geological Survey. He is a member of the Bar in the District of Columbia and State of Montana. He received degrees in geological engineering and professional engineering from the Montana School of Mines and a juris doctorate degree from Georgetown Law Center.

W. STELL HUIE, Partner, Huie, Ware, Sterne, Brown & Ide, Atlanta, Georgia. Mr. Huie is general counsel to the Metropolitan Atlanta Rapid Transit Authority and Georgia Bankers Association, past president of the Atlanta Bar Association and State Bar Association of Georgia, member of the American Bar Association (General Practice Section, National Legal Aid and Defender Association, Local Government Section, Urban Public and Private Transportation Committee), and fellow of the American Bar Foundation. He received a LL.B. degree from Emory University Law School.

M. G. JOHNSON, Counsel, Bechtel Power Corporation, Bechtel Corporation, San Francisco, California. Mr. Johnson joined the firm in 1964 and assumed his present position in 1976. He formerly served as attorney for Peter Kiewit Sons' and was involved in all legal aspects of domestic and international engineering and construction. He is a member of the State Bar of California, the American Bar Association and the Atomic Industry Forum Lawyers Committee, the Price-Anderson Committee, the Insurance Committee, and the American Institute of Chemical Engineers Executive and Engineering and Contracting Committee. He received a libral arts degree from Ohio Wesleyan and a juris doctorate degree from the University of Michigan.

JOHN R. LITTLE, JR., Regional Solicitor, U.S. Department of Interior, Denver, Colorado. Mr. Little has specialized in public contract law for 17 years. He joined the Department's Denver Regional Office in 1956 and held the position of assistant regional solicitor, Division of Contracts and Labor, from 1969 to 1974. He received a bachelor of arts degree and an LL.B. degree from the University of Colorado.

DARRELL P. MCCRORY, Partner, Monteleone and McCrory, Los Angeles, California. Mr. McCrory joined the law firm in 1955 and represents engineering contractors, public agencies, and surety companies in legal matters arising from engineering construction projects. He formerly served as deputy city attorney for the City of Los Angeles and represented the City's Department of Water and Power in litigation arising from water and power construction projects. He received a degree in philosophy from the University of Wisconsin and a juris doctorate degree from Stanford University.

LARRY S. MCREYNOLDS, Partner, Stokes and Shapiro, Atlanta, Georgia. Mr. McReynolds specializes in constitutional, construction, corporation, and labor law. He formerly was a nuclear engineer with McDonnell Douglas Corporation and Brown Engineering Company. He is a member of the American Bar Association, State Bar of Georgia, Atlanta Bar Association, and Colorado Bar Association. He received a degree in nuclear engineering from Kansas State University and a juris doctorate degree from the University of Denver.

RALPH NASH, Professor of Law, The National Law Center, George Washington University, Washington, D.C. Mr. Nash specializes in government procurement law and formerly served as the University's associate dean for graduate studies. He also serves several government agencies and private corporations as a consultant on government contract matters and previously served as contract negotiator for the Navy Department and with private industry in contract management and as counsel. He is active in the American and Federal Bar Associations and is a member of the Board of Advisors of the National Contract Management Association. He received a bachelor of arts degree from Princeton University and a juris doctorate degree from George Washington Law School.

ROBERT A. RUBIN, Esq., PE, Partner, Max E. Greenberg, Trayman, Cantor, Reiss & Blasky, New York, New York. Mr. Rubin specializes in construction contract documents, construction claims, and state and local government contract law. He is a member of the Construction Industry Arbitration Panel of the American Arbitration Association, vice chairman of the Committee on Contract Administration and past secretary of Executive Committee of the American Society of Civil Engineers Construction Division, and member of the New York County Lawyers Association and New York State and American Bar Associations. He received a degree in civil engineering from Cornell University and a juris doctorate degree from Columbia University.

Regulatory

DESLOGE BROWN, FASCE, Chief, Inspection Branch, Licensed Projects Division, Bureau of Power, Federal Power Commission, Washington, D.C. Mr. Brown, a registered professional engineer in several states, joined the Commission in 1968 and is responsible for staff supervision of hydroelectric project inspection activities of the five FPC regional offices. He formerly served as an officer in U.S. Army Corps of Engineers and has 30 years experience in a wide range of assignments related to topographic mapping, research and development of military engineering equipment, equipment maintenance, military construction and civil works programs. He is a member of the U.S. Committee on Large Dams and received degrees in civil engineering from the U.S. Military Academy and from Cornell University.

ROGER S. BOYD, Director, Division of Project Management, Office of Nuclear Reactor Regulation, Nuclear Regulatory Power Commission, Washington, D.C. Mr. Boyd joined the former Atomic Energy Commission in 1961 and was responsible for conducting safety evaluations of reactors; he became branch chief in 1964, assistant director in 1967, deputy director in 1973, and division director in 1976. He formerly was responsible for reactor safety analysis in the Battelle Memorial Institute Systems Engineering Division. He received a degree in physics from Ohio State University.

WILLIAM DICKERSON, Assistant Director, Office of Federal Activities (OFA) for Resource Development Staff, U.S. Environmental Protection Agency, Washington, D.C. Mr. Dickerson joined the OFA in 1972 as technical coordinator for development of environmental impact statement (EIS) review and guidelines and is responsible for office liaison with federal agencies engaged in natural resource and energy development such as Department of Interior, Department of Agriculture,

Federal Energy Administration, Energy Research and Development Administration, and Federal Power Commission. He received degrees in mechanical engineering from Kansas State University and aeronautics and astronautics from the University of Washington.

Public

BRENT BLACKWELDER, Chairman, League of Conservation Voters, Washington Representative, Environmental Policy Center, and Chairman of the Board, American Rivers Conservation Council, Washington, D.C. Having worked to organize these organizations, Mr. Blackwelder specializes in the water resource projects of the U.S. Army Corps of Engineers, the Bureau of Reclamation, the Tennessee Valley Authority, and the Soil Conservation Service and has monitored and testified on the programs of these agencies for over five years. He received a bachelor of arts degree from Duke University, a degree in mathematics from Yale University, and a degree in philosophy from the University of Maryland.

CELIA L. EPTING, Staff Specialist in Environmental Quality, League of Women Voters Education Fund, Washington, D.C. Ms. Epting's responsibilities include research and writing on environmental issues and analysis and preparation of comments on proposed federal regulations. She formerly served as a research assistant at the Florida Resources and Environmental Analysis Center involved in the development of a methodology for assessing socioeconomic and environmental impacts of nuclear power plants on local communities. She received degrees in the liberal arts and urban and regional planning from Florida State University.

PHILIP MAUSE, Partner, Nathan, Mause & Thorpe, Washington, D.C. Mr. Mause is an authority on electric utility rate matters. He formerly served as staff attorney for the Environmental Defense Fund (1974-1977). He received LL.B. and MPP degrees from Harvard University and a bachelor of arts degree from Georgetown University.

MARC MESSING, Director, Energy Facility Siting, Environmental Policy Institute, Washington, D.C., and lobbyist for the Environmental Policy Center on issues related to energy facility siting. Mr. Messing formerly worked on energy conservation and facility siting for the Friends of the Earth and served as director of the New York State Energy Coalition, legislative director of the New York State Environmental Planning Lobby, executive director of the Scientists' Institute for Public Information, and acting chairman of the National Clean Air Coalition. He received degrees in history and philosophy from the University of Chicago.

NEAL POTTER, President, Metropolitan Washington Council of Governments, Rockville, Maryland. Mr. Potter also is a member of the Transportation Planning and Metropolitan Planning Boards, the Montgomery County Maryland Council, and National Association of Counties' Environmental Quality and Education Committees. He formerly served as a research associate with Resources for the Future, Inc., and is past president of the Montgomery County Citizens Planning Association and chairman of the County Council Transportation Committee. He received degrees in economics and political science from the University of Minnesota and the University of Chicago.

146